What Office Tenants Want

1999 BOMA/ULI Office Tenant Survey Report

BOMA INTERNATIONAL

Urban Land Institute

About the Building Owners and Managers Association (BOMA) International

Founded in 1907, the Building Owners and Managers Association (BOMA) International is a dynamic international federation of more than 100 local associations. The 17,000 members of BOMA International own or manage more than 6 billion square feet of downtown and suburban commercial properties and facilities in North America and abroad. The mission of BOMA International is to advance the performance of commercial real estate through advocacy, professional competency, high standards, and research. For more information, visit the BOMA International Web site at www.boma.org.

W.S. (Bill) Garland
President
BOMA International

About ULI–the Urban Land Institute

ULI–the Urban Land Institute is a nonprofit education and research institute that is supported and directed by it members. Its mission is to provide responsible leadership in the use of land in order to enhance the total environment.

ULI sponsors educational programs and forums to encourage an open international exchange of ideas and sharing of experience; initiates research that anticipates emerging land use trends and issues and proposes creative solutions based on that research; provides advisory services; and publishes a wide variety of materials to disseminate information on land use and development.

Established in 1936, the Institute today has more than 14,000 members and associates from 60 countries, representing the entire spectrum of land use and development disciplines.

Richard M. Rosan
President
ULI–the Urban Land Institute

Recommended bibliographic listing:
Building Owners and Managers Association (BOMA) International and ULI–the Urban Land Institute. *What Office Tenants Want: 1999 BOMA/ULI Office Tenant Survey Report.* Washington, D.C.: BOMA International and ULI–the Urban Land Institute, 1999.

BOMA Catalog Number: 159-TENANT-693
ULI Catalog Number: OT1
International Standard Book Number: 0-87420-866-1
Library of Congress Catalog Card Number: 98-83051

Cover photo: Stockley Park; courtesy of Stockley Park Consortium Ltd.

Project Staff

Rachelle L. Levitt
Publisher
Senior Vice President, Policy and Practice
ULI–the Urban Land Institute

Gerard L. Lederer
Vice President, Government and Industry Affairs
BOMA International

Gayle Berens
Vice President, Real Estate Development Practice
ULI–the Urban Land Institute

Jo Allen Gause
Director, Office and Industrial Development
Project Co-Director
ULI–the Urban Land Institute

Matthew Bond
Director of Research
Project Co-Director
BOMA International

Anita Kramer
Anita Kramer & Associates
Project Analysis

Nancy H. Stewart
Director, Book Program
Managing Editor
ULI–the Urban Land Institute

Barbara M. Fishel
Editech
Manuscript Editor

Helene Y. Redmond
HYR Graphics
Book Design and Layout

Betsy Van Buskirk
Art Director
Cover Design
ULI–the Urban Land Institute

Kim Rusch
Graphic Artist

Diann Stanley-Austin
Associate Director of Publishing Operations
ULI–the Urban Land Institute

Contents

Preface v

Acknowledgments vii

1. **Introduction** 1

The Survey 2
Highlights of Results 4

2. **Profile of Respondents** 9

3. **Features, Amenities, and Services** 17

Locational Features 18
General Building Features 22
Features of Building Exterior 26
Features of Interior Common Areas 29
Features of Tenants' Office Suites 31
Building Amenities and Services 35
Building Management 38

4. **Intelligent Building Features** 41

5. **Alternative Office Strategies** 51

6. **Highlights by Type of Tenant** 61

Financial Services 62
Legal Services 63
Real Estate Firms 64

Planning/Architecture Firms 65
High-Tech Firms 66
Communications Firms 67
Insurance Firms 68
Medical Services 69
Nonprofit Organizations 69
Retail Tenants 70
Consulting Firms 71
Government Agencies 71
Engineering Firms 72
Accounting Firms 73

Appendix A **Survey Questionnaire** **75**

Appendix B **Preferences for Features, Amenities, and Services by Type of Business** **81**

Preface

This report, *What Office Tenants Want,* is the first collaboration between the Building Owners and Managers Association (BOMA) International and ULI–the Urban Land Institute, two organizations with similar missions—to provide responsible leadership to the real estate industry—but different emphases. ULI's range of interests covers the spectrum of land use and development, while BOMA is concerned primarily with the business of commercial properties once they are built. But BOMA's and ULI's interests converge on one major type of real estate—office buildings—and their interests in this segment of the real estate industry are complementary.

Any notion that office buildings lease and sell themselves was proved false in the overbuilt office market of the first half of the 1990s. Even in the relatively strong office market that prevails at the end of the decade, a huge base of space competes for tenants. The buildings that succeed in the foreseeable future will be those providing floor space and infrastructure that allow tenants to enhance their business performance and contribute to a productive work environment. But tenants consider more than just the space itself in their decisions to lease property; they are also looking for bottom-line value and services. Landlords must differentiate their buildings from the competition by offering superior services and amenities tailored to the building's occupants.

While most would agree that the key to attracting and keeping desirable tenants is to offer them the space and services they need, understanding what their preferences and requirements are is no easy matter. The goal of this survey of office tenants is to arm office building owners, developers, and managers with new insights about what office tenants want and what their priorities are.

BOMA and ULI members—property management companies, building owners, and developers—agreed to send the surveys to their tenants on behalf of the two organizations. It is hoped that the results of this survey will enable players across the entire spectrum of the office building industry—lenders, investors, architects, planners, developers, property managers, brokers, and others—to better meet the needs of tenants.

Acknowledgments

Many individuals and organizations contributed their time and talent to this survey and report. We would like to extend a very special thank you to the office building owners, developers, and managers who assisted in distributing the survey questionnaire to their tenants, in particular, the following companies, institutions, and associations: Allegis Realty Investors LLC, American Institute of Architects, Carr Real Estate Services, CB Richard Ellis, Charles E. Smith Companies, Chase Manhattan Bank, COMPASS Management & Leasing, Inc., Cushman & Wakefield, Inc., Daniels Associates, Inc., Equity Office Properties, First Union Corporation, Galbreath/LaSalle Partners, Glenborough Realty Trust, Inc., Grubb & Ellis Company, Heitman Properties Ltd., Hines, Hokanson Companies, Inc., Insignia Commercial Group, Inc., Julien J. Studley, Inc., Morlin Management Corporation, The Rouse Company, Tishman Speyer Properties, Trammell Crow Company, Transwestern Property Company, and TrizecHahn Office Properties. We extend special thanks also to the more than 1,800 office tenants who took the time to complete the survey; without their effort, we could not have produced this report.

Very special recognition and thanks must be given to Anita Kramer, principal, Anita Kramer & Associates, whose major contribution to all aspects of the project included developing the survey, analyzing data, and writing the report. She spent many hours analyzing voluminous data, patiently coaxing the story out of the numbers.

A number of ULI and BOMA staff members and consultants were also instrumental in this effort. Rachelle Levitt and Gayle Berens at ULI and Gerry Lederer at BOMA provided overall direction and support for the project. Jo Allen Gause at ULI and Matthew Bond at BOMA were the project's co-directors. Juanita Little and Arthur Hall at BOMA assisted in designing the survey, collecting and analyzing data, and helping with the numerous revisions to the manuscript. Ellen Ku, formerly with BOMA, was an integral part of designing and distributing the survey. ULI's production staff did an outstanding job of publishing the report in a very short period of time, and we greatly appreciate their quick response to our short deadline. Nancy Stewart oversaw the editing and production process. Barbara Fishel edited the text, Helene Redmond expertly designed and laid out the book, Kim Rusch produced many of the graphics, and Betsy Van Buskirk designed the cover.

Finally, our sincere thanks and appreciation go to the members of BOMA International's Research Committee and to ULI's Project Advisory and Policy and Practice Committees listed on the following pages for their hard work and insightful suggestions.

BOMA International Research Committee

Raymond McLaughlin, Chair
101 Hudson Leasing Associates
Jersey City, New Jersey

Larry Guilemette, Vice Chair
Samuels & Associates
Boston, Massachusetts

Janine Allen
Grubb & Ellis Management Services, Inc.
Denver, Colorado

Pamela Bearce
Chaney Brooks & Co.
Honolulu, Hawaii

Charles Brown
The Harris Group
Charlotte, North Carolina

David Ciechanowicz
CB Richard Ellis
Indianapolis, Indiana

David Corpening
The Keith Corp.
Charlotte, North Carolina

Lori Bryant Donovan
Tulsa Properties
Tulsa, Oklahoma

Kim Feken-Partin
Realty Operating Co.
Tulsa, Oklahoma

Patrick Fine
Reliance Development Group, Inc.
Denver, Colorado

Walt Flannery
Chevron Real Estate Management Co.
San Ramon, California

Peter Ford
General Services Administration
Washington, D.C.

Robert Freeman
West World Management Co.
Philadelphia, Pennsylvania

Susan Griffin
Griffin & McCormick
Oakland, California

Warren Herd
Wilcox Realty Group, Inc.
Dallas, Texas

Doug Jackson
CB Richard Ellis
Columbus, Ohio

Robert Keller
CB Richard Ellis
Detroit, Michigan

Todd Lewers
Apex Site Management
Bethesda, Maryland

Howard Lundeen
Landauer Associates, Inc.
Dallas, Texas

Tanda McMahon
Trammell Crow Company
Tulsa, Oklahoma

Janice Moss
Highwoods Properties, Inc.
Atlanta, Georgia

James Ruffini
Block & Co. Realtors
Kansas City, Missouri

Kathleen Coulter Smith
CB Richard Ellis
Tucson, Arizona

Donna Stewart
BOMA/Greater Hartford
Avon, Connecticut

Mary Youngman
Allied Plaza
La Mesa, California

ULI Project Advisory Committee

Barry Gruebbel
Crescent Real Estate Equities, Ltd.
Fort Worth, Texas

Michael Kasser*
Holualoa Arizona, Inc.
Tucson, Arizona

Charles McBride, Jr.
CB Richard Ellis
Los Angeles, California

Robert Ruth*
Tooley & Company
Los Angeles, California

*Also a member of the ULI Policy and Practice Committee.

ULI Policy and Practice Committee

Leanne Lachman, Chair
Schroder Real Estate Associates
New York, New York

Peter Rummell, Assistant Chair
The St. Joe Company
Jacksonville, Florida

William Barnes
Barnes and Company
San Francisco, California

Luis Belmonte
AMB Property Corporation
San Francisco, California

James Bond
Central Parking System
Nashville, Tennessee

James Curtis
Bristol Group, Inc.
San Francisco, California

Alice Early
Russell Reynolds Associates, Inc.
New York, New York

Michael Giliberto
J.P. Morgan Investment Management
New York, New York

Joseph Gyourko
Wharton Real Estate Center
University of Pennsylvania
Philadelphia, Pennsylvania

Louis Hoyes
Fannie Mae
Washington, D.C.

Kenneth Hughes
UC Urban
Dallas, Texas

Clyde Jackson
Wynne/Jackson, Inc.
Dallas, Texas

Robert Larson
Taubman Realty Group
Bloomfield Hills, Michigan

Randall Lewis
Lewis Homes Management Corporation
Upland, California

James Light
Chaffin/Light Associates
Snowmass Village, Colorado

Franklin Martin
Hidden Springs Community, L.L.C.
Boise, Idaho

Richard Michaux
Avalon Bay Communities, Inc.
Alexandria, Virginia

Ronald Nahas
Rafanelli and Nahas
Orinda, California

Richard Peiser
Harvard Graduate School of Design
Cambridge, Massachusetts

James Porter
Altoon + Porter Architects
Los Angeles, California

Lynne Sagalyn
Graduate School of Business
Columbia University
New York, New York

Michael Spies
Tishman Speyer Properties
London, England

Federico Stubbe
Stugo
San Juan, Puerto Rico

Daniel Van Epp
The Howard Hughes Corporation
Summerlin Division
Las Vegas, Nevada

Jon Wellhoefer
Milwaukee Redevelopment Corporation
Milwaukee, Wisconsin

Kenneth Wong
Walt Disney Imagineering
Glendale, California

Karl Zavitkovsky
NationsBanc Montgomery Securities, L.L.C.
Dallas, Texas

1 Introduction

The Survey

In an effort to determine what office tenants think are the most important features, amenities, and services in their office buildings, the Building Owners and Managers Association (BOMA) International and ULI–the Urban Land Institute collaborated on a survey. The questionnaire, sent to approximately 20,000 office tenants throughout the United States and Canada, requested opinions, evaluations, and information from tenants on three subjects—features and amenities of office buildings, intelligent building systems and structural features, and the use of alternative office strategies, such as telecommuting and hoteling (see Appendix A). It also asked tenants how satisfied they are with the features, amenities, and services in their present space. Slightly more than 1,800 responses were received, primarily from principals/owners, executives, office managers, or department managers of the responding companies, a response rate of 9 percent. *What Office Tenants Want* presents the results of the survey.

A primary goal of the survey was to learn more about the specific requirements of different types of tenants for office space, what features are the most and least important to them, how they expect their need for office space to change, and how satisfied they are with the office space they currently occupy. To those ends, the first section of the questionnaire asked tenants for some general information, including the type of business they operate, how much space they lease or own, and where the office is located (city and state or province, CBD or suburbs). The second section asked tenants to rate, on a numbered scale, the importance to their organization of 53 building features, amenities, and services, and then to rate their satisfaction with the availability, quality, or level of each item in their current building (Figure 1-1). The 53 features were grouped into seven categories on the survey form: locational features, general building features, features of building exterior, features of interior common areas, features of tenants' office suites, building amenities, and building management. ("Suburban location" and "downtown location," two of the 53 features, are not included as separate items in this analysis, but as identifying characteristics of respondents.)

Section III asked tenants to review a list of 13 "intelligent" features (fiber-optics capability, automatic sensors, for example) and indicate which ones are available in their current building. They were then asked to rank the three intelligent building features that are most important to their organization, specify any such features that their organization needs but are not available in their building, and indicate whether they would be willing to pay additional rent to have those features made available.

Photo credit for page 1
Offices of Sony Music International
Miami, Florida
Reproduced with permission from *Corporate Interiors No. 1*
Design Firm: TAS Design
Photography: Paul Warchol

Figure 1-1 Importance of and Satisfaction with Building Features, Amenities, and Services

	Important (Percent)	Satisfied (Percent)
Rental rates (including pass-throughs/escalations)	99	88
Comfortable temperature	99	74
Indoor air quality	99	81
Acoustics/noise control	99	83
Building management's ability to meet your needs	99	89
Quality of building maintenance work	99	89
Building management's responsiveness	99	89
Effectiveness of communications with building management	99	86
Appearance of building	98	93
Operating expenses	98	87
Appearance of grounds/landscaping	98	92
Appearance of entry lobby (style/finishes)	97	89
Buildingwide security systems after hours	97	85
Appearance of common areas other than lobby	97	84
Power capacity	97	93
Tenant control of temperature	96	65
Image and prestige of the building	95	92
On-site parking	94	80
Tenant improvement allowance	93	83
Security/controlled access	93	90
Proximity to restrooms	93	95
On-site building management staff	93	90
Flexible suite layout (e.g., easily reconfigured)	92	87
Cost of parking	91	75
Environmentally friendly building systems and materials	90	89
Cost of after-hours heating/cooling	89	79
Elevator service speed	88	72
On-site security guard	88	85
Buildingwide security systems during work day	88	85
Proximity to business services	87	98
Proximity to elevators	84	98
Proximity to where employees live	81	95
Proximity to restaurants/retail/personal services	81	94
Disabled access	78	92
Covered parking	77	77
Proximity to clients	76	98
Food service	75	71
Tenant mix	73	92
Outside signage for your organization	71	80
Banking/ATM	70	79
Proximity to public transportation	69	95
Convenience retail stores	64	81
Outside loading docks	53	82
Fitness center	53	58
Child-care facility	44	48
Concierge	41	77
Operable windows	40	61
Shared videoconference facility	38	60
Shared teleconference facility	34	64
Shared business services (e.g., data and word processing)	29	78
Roof-loading capacity	23	90

Notes: The numbers in the first column represent the percentage of respondents to whom a particular feature is important, that is, who rated it 3, 4, or 5 on the survey. For example, nearly all respondents (99 percent) think the first eight features are important, and at least 90 percent of respondents think the first 25 are important. The second column indicates how satisfied tenants are with the features. For example, although nearly all tenants think a comfortable temperature is important, only about three-quarters are satisfied with the temperature in their office space.

"Suburban location" and "downtown location," which were also on the questionnaire, are not included as separate features in this analysis, but as identifying characteristics of respondents.

Section IV asked tenants to indicate which, if any, of three alternative office strategies their company uses: hoteling (a practice in which employees who do not have a permanent desk can reserve space in the regular office by calling ahead), telecommuting (a practice that allows employees to work at home on a regular basis during normal business hours), and virtual office (the use of a personal computer with modem and fax capability, printer, and cellular telephone so employees can work in nontraditional settings, such as a client's office). Tenants were then asked to estimate what percentage of their employees participate in these programs and the top three reasons that they implemented each practice. The final question in this section concerned the impact of these alternatives on the amount and configuration of respondents' office space.

Highlights Of Results

Profile of Respondents

- Slightly more than 1,800 (1,829) tenants responded to the BOMA/ULI Office Tenant Survey from 126 metropolitan areas across the United States and Canada (see Chapter 2 for a full discussion). About half the respondents are located in central city locations, the remainder in suburban locations (suburban downtowns, office parks, and other suburban locations).

- Respondents represent more than 20 different types of businesses. The four largest groups are financial services, legal services, real estate, and planning/architecture (see Chapter 6 for a full discussion of tenant groups).

- More than half the responding tenants lease 5,000 or fewer square feet of office space, and close to 70 percent lease 10,000 or fewer square feet. More insurance and financial service firms occupy spaces of 10,000 to 60,000 square feet than other tenant groups, and more government agencies occupy spaces greater than 60,000 square feet.

- Half the tenants surveyed anticipate a change in the amount of space needed over the next three years, most of them an increase in space needed of 50 percent or less of current space.

- One-half the respondents are inclined to stay in their present building when the current lease expires. Thirty-six percent are undecided, and 14 percent say they are not inclined to stay.

- A large majority of respondents are satisfied with the length of their lease. Still, 34 percent of respondents would change the length of their lease were they able to renegotiate it today; 22 percent would want a shorter lease, 12 percent a longer one.

Office Building Features, Amenities, And Services

- The most important features, amenities, and services to the responding tenants are related to the comfort and quality of indoor air, the acoustics, and the quality of the building management's service (see Chapter 3 for a full discussion). Ninety percent or more of respondents give the following six features a rating of very important (that is, 5 on the survey): comfortable temperature (95 percent), indoor air quality (94 percent), quality of building maintenance work (93 percent), building management's responsiveness (92 percent), building management's ability to meet the tenant's needs (92 percent), and acoustics/noise control (90 percent). Eighty-seven percent of respondents also rate the effectiveness of communications with building management very important.

- The vast majority of respondents say that rental rates (89 percent), operating expenses (86 percent), and after-hours security (89 percent) are among their highest priorities for office space. Security/controlled access to their office suite, the presence of an on-site security guard, and the presence of on-site building management staff are also very important to most tenants (79 percent, 76 percent, and 79 percent, respectively).

- Tenants want their buildings to look good inside and out and to convey the right image. Respondents rate several items on the survey related to a building's appearance as very important: appearance of the building's exterior (86 percent), appearance of the entry lobby (86 percent), appearance of other common areas (82 percent), and appearance of the grounds (82 percent). Seventy-seven percent say a building's image and prestige are of the highest importance to them.

- It will come as no surprise to office building developers and managers that parking is a matter of utmost importance to tenants. Eighty-five percent of respondents say the availability of on-site parking is very important in their evaluation of office space, and 78 percent say the cost of parking is one of their highest priorities. Only 58 percent rate covered parking as a primary concern, although an additional 19 percent say this feature is of some importance to them.

- In their own office suite in addition to good indoor air quality, acoustics, and a comfortable temperature, the majority of respondents (85 percent) say that it is very important for them to be able to control the temperature level in their own suite. Most respondents (65 percent) also deem a reasonable cost of using the HVAC (heating, ventilation, air-conditioning) system after hours very important.

- It is somewhat surprising that the least important issues to responding tenants are many building amenities and certain building features, such as outside signage and operable windows. In fact, no more than 50 percent assign any importance whatsoever to child-care facilities, a concierge, and shared business facilities. Slightly more tenants are interested in a fitness center (53 percent). Respondents find food service, proximity to convenience and retail stores, and the availability of banking/ATM the most important amenities. The message to owners and managers should be to understand what building amenities are most useful to the specific types of tenants they wish to attract and keep (see Appendix B).

- Since more than half of respondents give some degree of importance (that is, 3, 4, or 5 on the survey) to 46 of the 51 building features, amenities, and services rated in the survey, it is interesting to note that 80 to 90 percent of respondents have been able to find office space that satisfies most of their primary requirements. The two notable exceptions are related to air temperature and parking. Nearly a quarter of respondents are dissatisfied with the temperature in their office, and an even greater number (35 percent) are not satisfied with their ability to control the temperature in their office suite. And 25 percent of tenants are dissatisfied with the cost of parking in or near their building.

- Building developers, owners, and managers should take note: Tenants' ability to control the temperature in their suite is the only feature to show up on both the list of most important features and the list of items where tenants are least satisfied. To make an immediate and positive impact on tenants' perception of a building, landlords and managers could focus on temperature-related functions by updating HVAC systems so that tenants can control the temperature in their suite or by helping tenants make better use of their existing system.

- Although respondents, taken as a whole, are relatively satisfied that the features and services available in their current building meet their key requirements, some variations are apparent among types of tenants. For example, users of large office spaces are far more satisfied than tenants in the smallest spaces with indoor air quality, acoustics/noise control, the ability to attain a comfortable temperature, and tenants' control of temperature. The differences are most pronounced between tenants in spaces over 100,000 square feet and those in spaces under 10,000 square feet.

Intelligent Building Features

- Only 56 percent of all respondents are located in buildings with any of the 13 intelligent building features listed in the survey (see Chapter 4 for a full discussion). Intelligent features related to computer and communications functions are the most commonly available, with built-in wiring for access to the Internet (found in 25 percent of respondents' buildings) the most prevalent feature. Intelligent building systems and structural features are far less common, found in no more than 12 percent of buildings, with one notable exception. High-tech, energy-efficient HVAC systems are found in 23 percent of respondents' buildings.

- Six intelligent building features are consistently among the top rated: HVAC systems, wiring for the Internet, wiring for high-speed networks, LAN (local-area network) and WAN (wide-area network) connectivity, fiber-optics capability, and conduits for power/data/voice cabling. The high ranking of HVAC systems underscores the importance tenants place on comfortable temperature and on being able to control their own temperature.

- Just because an intelligent building feature is available in an office building does not mean tenants will deem it important. Building owners and managers should make sure that the tenants they wish to attract and keep really need or want a particular feature or technology before providing it.

- Tenant groups vary widely in their use of intelligent features. High-tech, insurance, and financial service firms, and government agencies are more often located in buildings with intelligent systems than any of the other business groups. Owner-occupied buildings are twice as likely to have any intelligent features as buildings with leased space. Far more large employers and space users occupy buildings with intelligent features than smaller tenants.

- The intelligent features respondents mention most frequently as needed by their organization but not available in their building are telecommunications capability (access to cable TV, fiber-optics capability, videoconferencing, satellite access), an energy-efficient, tenant-controlled HVAC system, a controlled-access security system with monitoring, and a redundant power source.

- Most tenants (72 percent) who need intelligent features that are not available in their building say they would be willing to pay additional rent to have the features made available.

Alternative Office Strategies

- Only 33 percent of respondents have implemented any of the alternative office strategies mentioned in the survey (see Chapter 5 for a full discussion). Telecommuting is the most popular strategy, with 24 percent of tenants using it. Some 18 percent of respondents use a virtual office, while only 7 percent use hoteling.

- Although one-third of responding tenants have adopted an alternative strategy, their employees' participation rate is relatively low (10 to 15 percent).

- Most companies implement alternative office strategies in response to demand from their employees and to increase operating efficiency. Respondents that have adopted telecommuting note both these reasons. Virtual offices are implemented primarily as a means to increase efficiency, while hoteling is used to increase efficiency and to reduce the amount of office space needed.

- Only about 25 percent of tenants that use telecommuting or virtual offices report a change in the total amount of space needed. Hoteling has a greater impact on total space needed than other forms of nontraditional office practices mentioned in the survey; 45 percent of those who use hoteling report it has had an effect on the amount of space they need. Most changes in space requirements have been to reduce total space needed, but a small component (4 to 7 percent) has actually needed more space.

- The use of alternative office strategies has affected the way tenants configure their office space in about the same proportions as the total demand for space. Most frequently, the changes have involved fewer private offices and more "team space" and open-plan work areas. More than 30 percent of respondents using an alternative office strategy report making greater use of telecommunications technology as a result of the change.

- High-tech, insurance, accounting, and consulting firms are among the top users of alternative office strategies. Almost 50 percent of tenants who categorize their organizations as high-tech say they use telecommuting, 37 percent use virtual offices, and 15 percent use hoteling.

2

Profile of Respondents

This chapter presents a profile of the 1,829 office tenants who responded to the BOMA/ULI survey (Figure 2-1).

- *Tenants represent 20 different types of businesses plus one "other."* The four largest business groups are financial services, legal services, real estate, and planning/architecture.

- *The number of employees per tenant ranges from fewer than ten to more than 1,000 persons.* Sixty-eight percent of all tenants have fewer than 20 employees.

- *Tenants occupy office spaces ranging from under 1,000 square feet to more than 250,000 square feet.* The largest group of tenants by far occupies space between 1,000 and 5,000 square feet. Over 50 percent of all tenants lease 5,000 or fewer square feet, and close to 70 percent lease 10,000 or fewer square feet.

  Although the amount of space leased ranges widely in all types of businesses, relatively more retailers, medical services, and planning/architecture firms are in spaces of 10,000 or fewer square feet, more engineering firms are in spaces of 10,000 to 20,000 square feet, more insurance and financial firms are in spaces of 20,000 to 60,000 square feet, and more government agencies are in spaces greater than 60,000 square feet.

- *Most tenants occupy Class A and Class B buildings.* Over 30 percent rate their buildings as Class A, almost 60 percent as Class B. Respondents rated their buildings according to descriptions provided on the survey form. *Prime buildings,* referred to here as Class A, offer luxury amenities, high-quality standard finishes, state-of-the-art systems, exceptional accessibility, and a definite presence. *Average buildings,* referred to here as Class B, offer basic amenities, fair- to good-quality finishes, and standard systems. *Below-average buildings,* referred to here as Class C, are dated, offer few amenities, and emphasize function.

- *Tenants are equally divided between those that anticipate a change in the amount of space needed over the next three years and those that do not.* Almost all who anticipate a change foresee an increase in space needed of 50 percent or less of current space. Only 8 percent anticipate a decrease in space required.

  Given the move to downsize and/or consolidate government operations, 21 percent of government agencies anticipate a decrease in space required; only 36 percent anticipate an increase over the next three years. Far more high-tech firms (59 percent), on the other hand, anticipate an increase in the amount of space required.

Photo credit for page 9
Reproduced with permission from *Corporate Interiors No. 1*
Design Firm: Perkins & Will
Photography: Marco Lorenzetti, Hedrich Blessing

Figure 2-1 **Profile of Respondents**

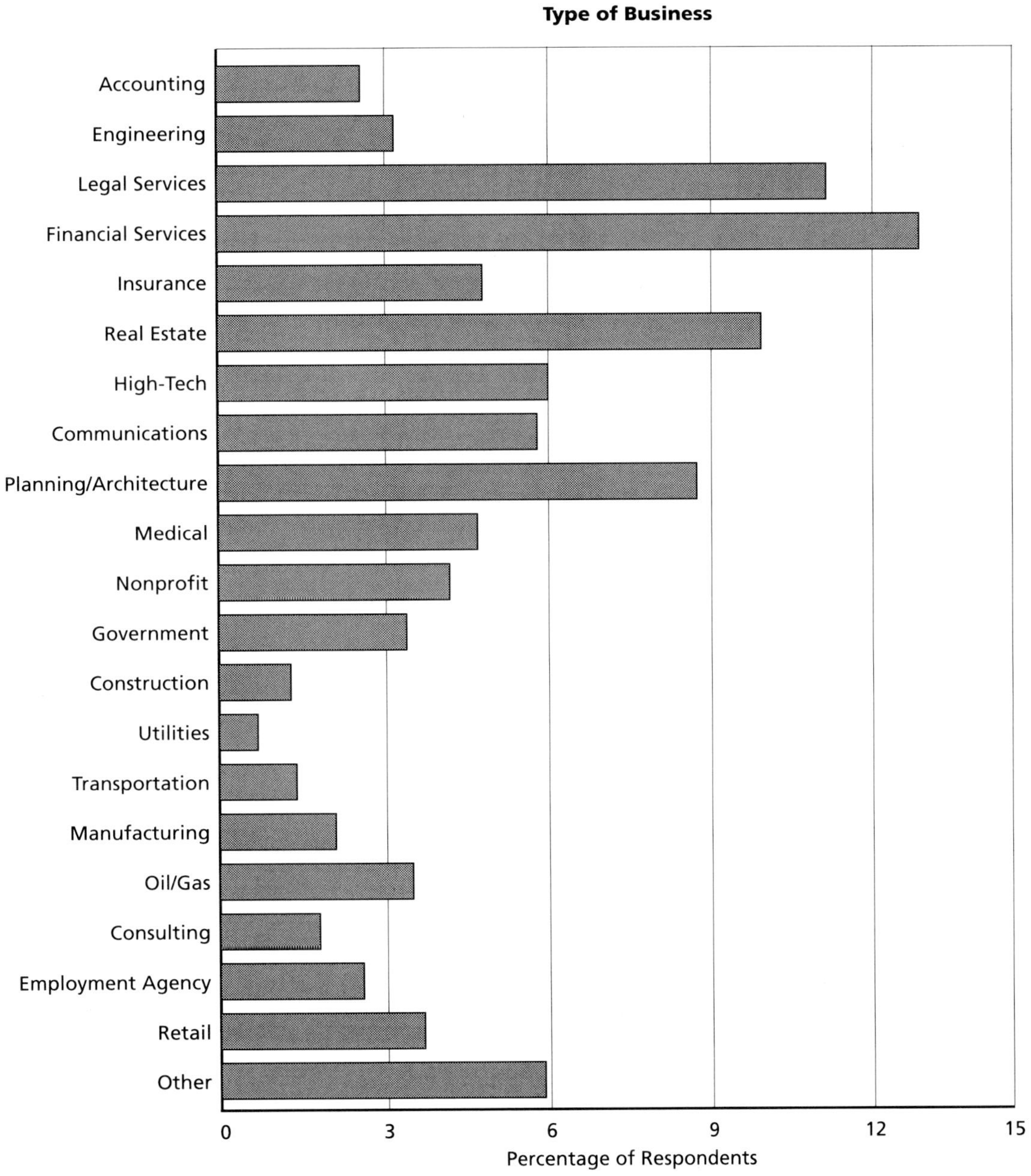

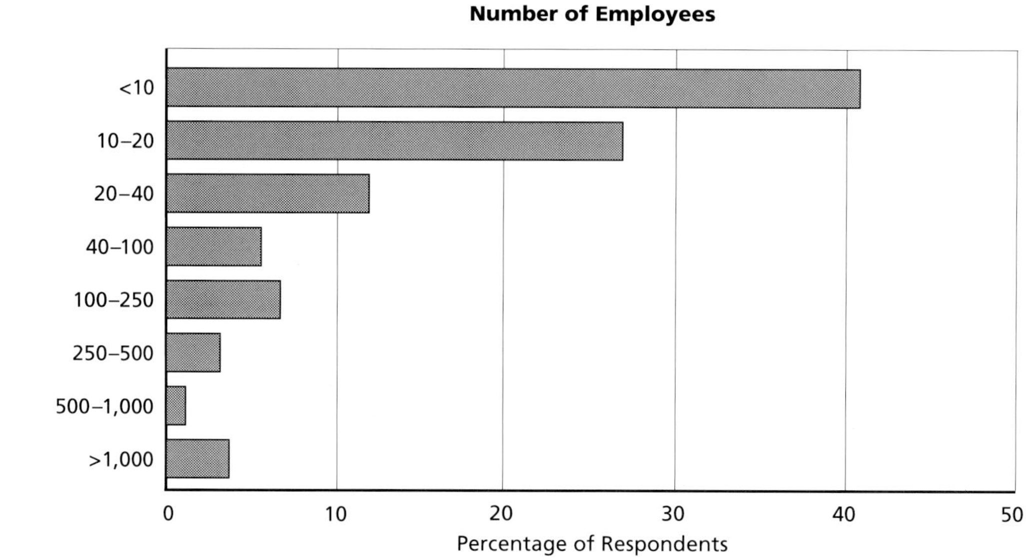
Number of Employees
<10
10–20
20–40
40–100
100–250
250–500
500–1,000
>1,000
0
10
20
30
40
50
Percentage of Respondents

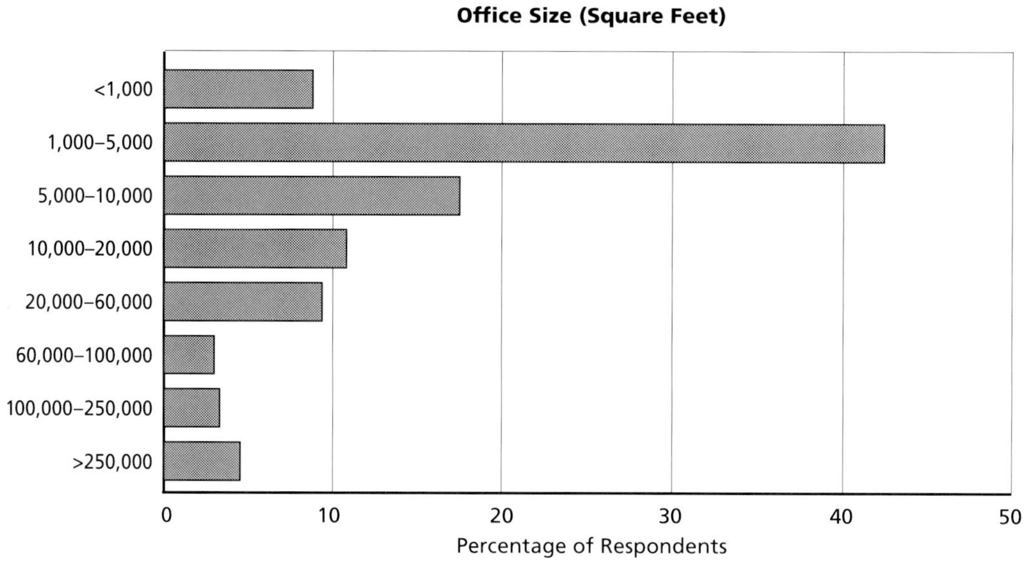
Office Size (Square Feet)
<1,000
1,000–5,000
5,000–10,000
10,000–20,000
20,000–60,000
60,000–100,000
100,000–250,000
>250,000
0
10
20
30
40
50
Percentage of Respondents

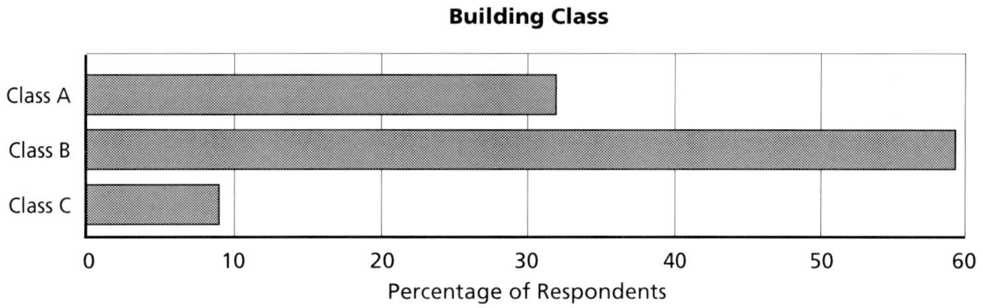
Building Class
Class A
Class B
Class C
0
10
20
30
40
50
60
Percentage of Respondents

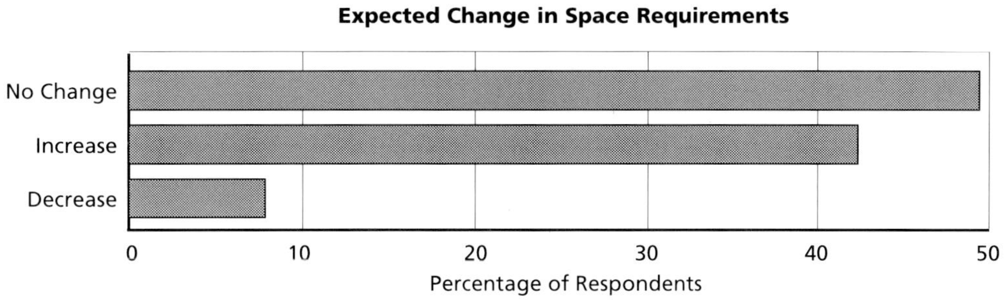
Expected Change in Space Requirements
No Change
Increase
Decrease
0
10
20
30
40
50
Percentage of Respondents

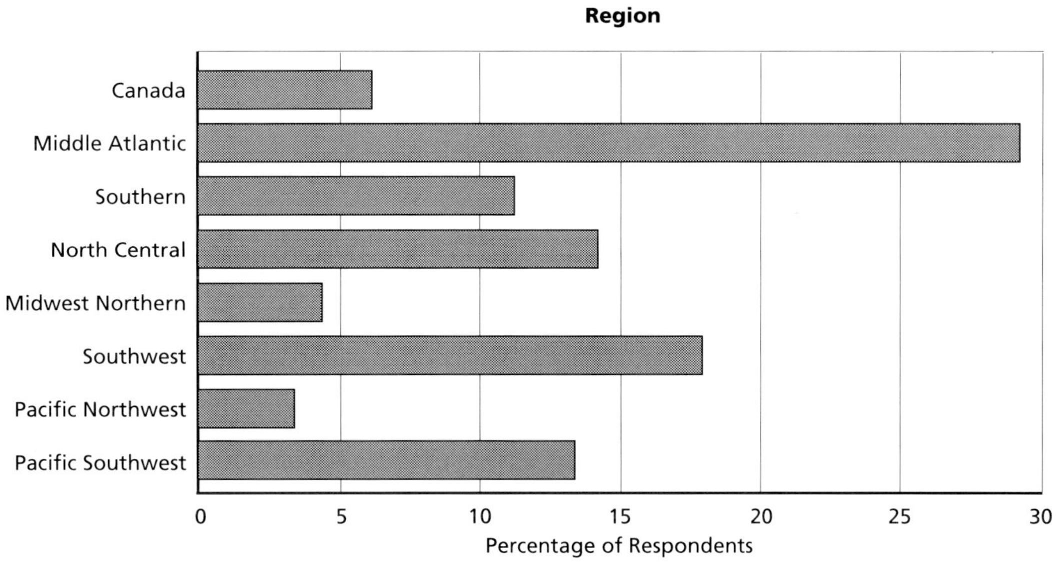
Region
Canada
Middle Atlantic
Southern
North Central
Midwest Northern
Southwest
Pacific Northwest
Pacific Southwest
0
5
10
15
20
25
30
Percentage of Respondents

 Profile of Respondents (continued)

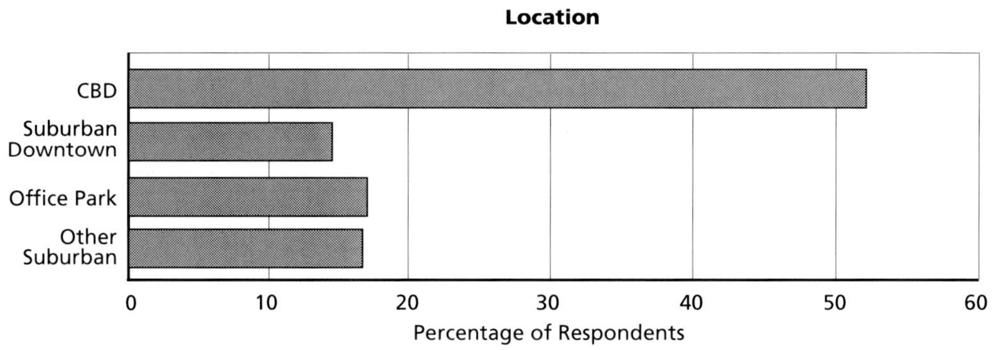

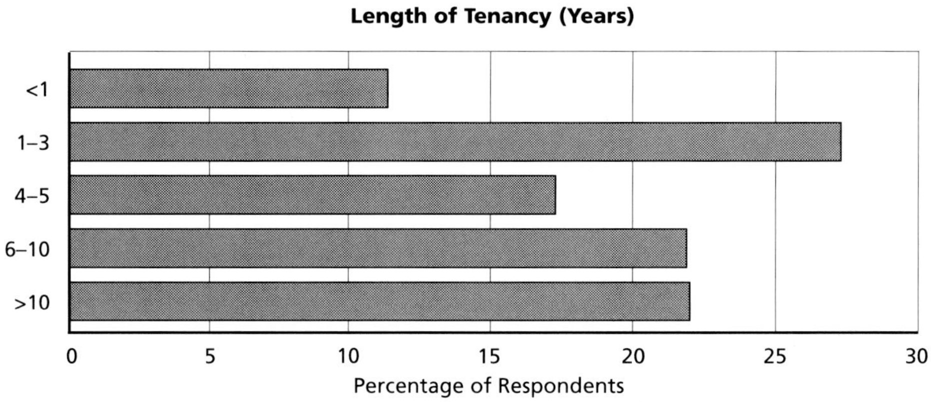

- *One-half of respondents are inclined to stay in their present building when the current lease expires.* Thirty-six percent are undecided, and 14 percent say they are *not* inclined to stay.

- *Respondents are from across the United States and Canada* (Figure 2-2). The largest group by far comes from the Middle Atlantic states.

- *Respondents are located in 126 metropolitan areas.* Metropolitan areas with the largest number of responses are Washington, D.C., Chicago, Houston, Dallas, Philadelphia, Baltimore, Honolulu, Los Angeles, Pittsburgh, Austin, Seattle, Atlanta, Indianapolis, Charlotte, St. Louis, Toronto, Las Vegas, Calgary, Miami, and New York.

Figure 2-2 **Regions Used in the BOMA/ULI Survey**

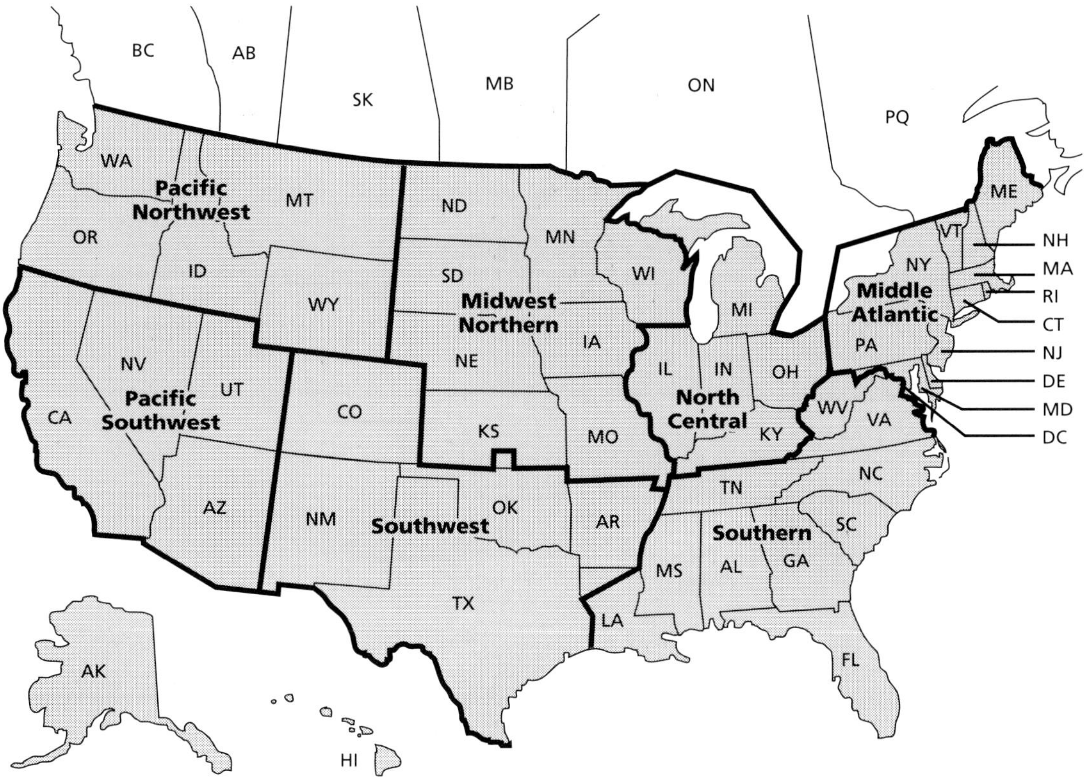

* *Tenants are almost equally divided between central city and suburban locations.* Just over half the tenants are located in central city downtowns, with the balance in three suburban locations—suburban downtowns, office parks, and other suburban locations. Certain types of businesses are more concentrated in a single location: legal services (82 percent), nonprofits (70 percent), and communications firms (62 percent) tend to be located in central city downtowns.

* *Tenants have generally occupied their office space for at least one year;* over 60 percent of tenants have been in their present location for four or more years.

* *Tenants tend to lease rather than own office space*—93 percent and 7 percent, respectively.

Figure 2-3 **Respondents' Job Functions**

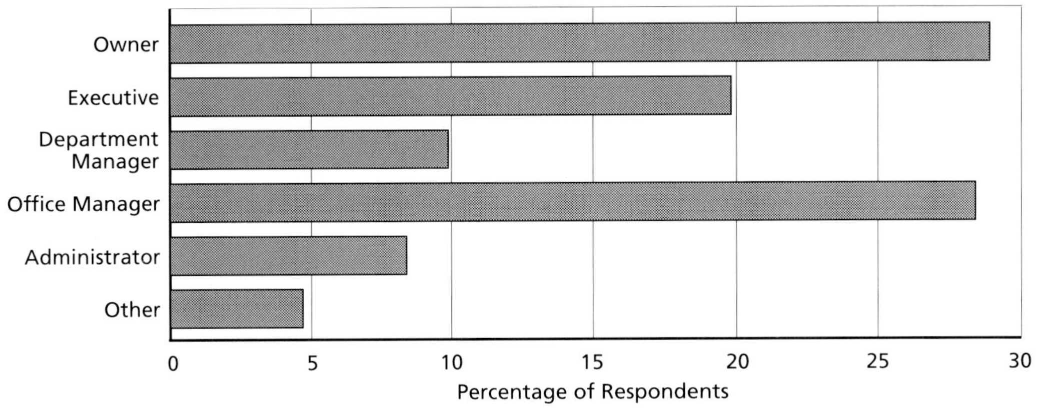

- *Only 15 percent of respondents sublease some of their space to another tenant.*

- *A large majority of tenants are satisfied with the length of their lease.* Still, 34 percent of respondents would change the length of their lease were they able to renegotiate it today; 22 percent would want a shorter lease, 12 percent a longer one.

- *A large majority of tenants do not care about an expansion provision or sublease clause in their lease.* Still, 31 percent would want a provision for expansion and 8 percent a sublease clause if they could renegotiate the lease.

- *Respondents most often hold the titles principal/owner and office manager* (Figure 2-3).

3

Features, Amenities, And Services

This chapter reports on the relative importance to tenants of the 51 building features, amenities, and services shown in Figure 3-1 (grouped in seven categories), and their satisfaction with the availability, quality, or level of each feature. Respondents recorded their ratings on a scale of 1 to 5.

The chapter discusses the findings separately for each of the seven categories. Each discussion of findings focuses on all tenants and then highlights any differences in ratings among various tenants by demographic characteristics. Figure 3-1 summarizes the responses by category of feature. Numbers in the first column represent the percentage of respondents to whom a particular feature is important. ("Important" as used in this discussion refers to the combination of "important" and "very important" on the pie charts and graphs.) The second column indicates the percentage of respondents who are "satisfied" and "very satisfied" with a particular feature.

Locational Features

Tenants rated the relative importance to their organization of seven locational features and their satisfaction with each one. Two of the features describe a tenant's location in a downtown or a suburban setting, and the other five describe the tenant's proximity to business and personal amenities outside the office building. The locational features rated in the survey include:

- Downtown location
- Suburban location
- Proximity to clients
- Proximity to business services
- Proximity to restaurants/retail/personal services
- Proximity to public transportation
- Proximity to where employees live.

The importance of a downtown or suburban location is presented only for respondents who are currently in that location (Figure 3-2). Tenants whose offices are now in central city downtowns view their location as a valuable asset; it is one of the most highly rated features in the entire survey, with 94 percent of central city tenants indicating their downtown location is important.

Photo credit for page 17
AmSouth Bancorporation
Birmingham, Alabama
Reproduced with permission from *Corporate Interiors No. 1*
Design Firm: Lehman|Smith|Wiseman & Associates
Photography: Jon Miller, Hedrich Blessing

Figure 3-1

Importance of and Satisfaction with Building Features, Amenities, and Services, by Category

	Important (Percent)	Satisfied (Percent)
Locational Features		
Proximity to business services	87	98
Proximity to where employees live	81	95
Proximity to restaurants/retail/personal services	81	94
Proximity to clients	76	98
Proximity to public transportation	69	95
General Building Features		
Rental rates (including pass-throughs/escalations)	99	88
Operating expenses	98	87
Image and prestige of the building	95	92
On-site parking	94	80
Tenant improvement allowance	93	83
Cost of parking	91	75
Environmentally friendly building systems and materials	90	89
Disabled access	78	92
Covered parking	77	77
Tenant mix	73	92
Features of Building Exterior		
Appearance of building	98	93
Appearance of grounds/landscaping	98	92
Outside signage for your organization	71	80
Outside loading docks	53	82
Operable windows	40	61
Roof-loading capacity	23	90
Features of Interior Common Areas		
Appearance of entry lobby (style/finishes)	97	89
Buildingwide security systems after hours	97	85
Appearance of common areas other than lobby	97	84
Elevator service speed	88	72
Buildingwide security systems during work day	88	85
Features of Tenants' Office Suites		
Comfortable temperature	99	74
Indoor air quality	99	81
Acoustics/noise control	99	83
Power capacity	97	93
Tenant control of temperature	96	65
Security/controlled access	93	90
Proximity to restrooms	93	95
Flexible suite layout (e.g., easily reconfigured)	92	87
Cost of after-hours heating/cooling	89	79
Proximity to elevators	84	98
Building Amenities		
Food service	75	71
Banking/ATM	70	79
Convenience retail stores	64	81
Fitness center	53	58
Child-care facility	44	48
Concierge	41	77
Shared videoconference facility	38	60
Shared teleconference facility	34	64
Shared business services (e.g., data and word processing)	29	78
Building Management		
Quality of building maintenance work	99	89
Building management's ability to meet your needs	99	89
Building management's responsiveness	99	89
Effectiveness of communications with building management	99	86
On-site building management staff	93	90
On-site security guard	88	85

Figure 3-2 **Importance of Existing Location**

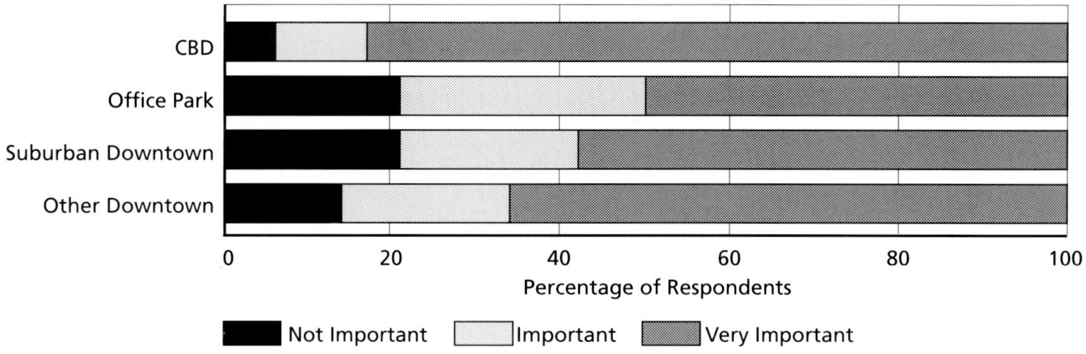

In contrast, 79 percent of tenants whose offices are in suburban downtowns and office parks view their suburban location as important. A downtown suburban location is apparently not a substitute for a central city downtown. Tenants in suburban downtowns view their suburban location as far more important than their location in a downtown, with only 45 percent of those tenants indicating that a location in a downtown is important.

Despite the variations in importance, tenants in central city downtowns and all suburban locations are overwhelmingly satisfied with their location.

The features of proximity to outside businesses and personal amenities are among the lower-rated ones in the survey (Figure 3-3). Ratings range from 87 percent of tenants who deem proximity to business services important to 69 percent who deem proximity to public transportation important. Moreover, these issues involving proximity are among the most highly rated of all features in the entire survey in terms of satisfaction.

- Proximity to particular businesses and personal amenities outside their office building is more important to some tenants than to others:
  - *Proximity to clients* is more important to tenants in accounting firms, medical services, retailers, and legal services than to tenants in other types of businesses. This feature is least important to nonprofit organizations.
  - *Proximity to business services* is more important to tenants in accounting firms than to tenants in other types of businesses. It is the least important to tenants in medical services.
  - *Proximity to where employees live* is more important to tenants in engineering firms and least important to retailers and medical services.

Figure 3-3 **Proximity to Outside Businesses and Personal Amenities**

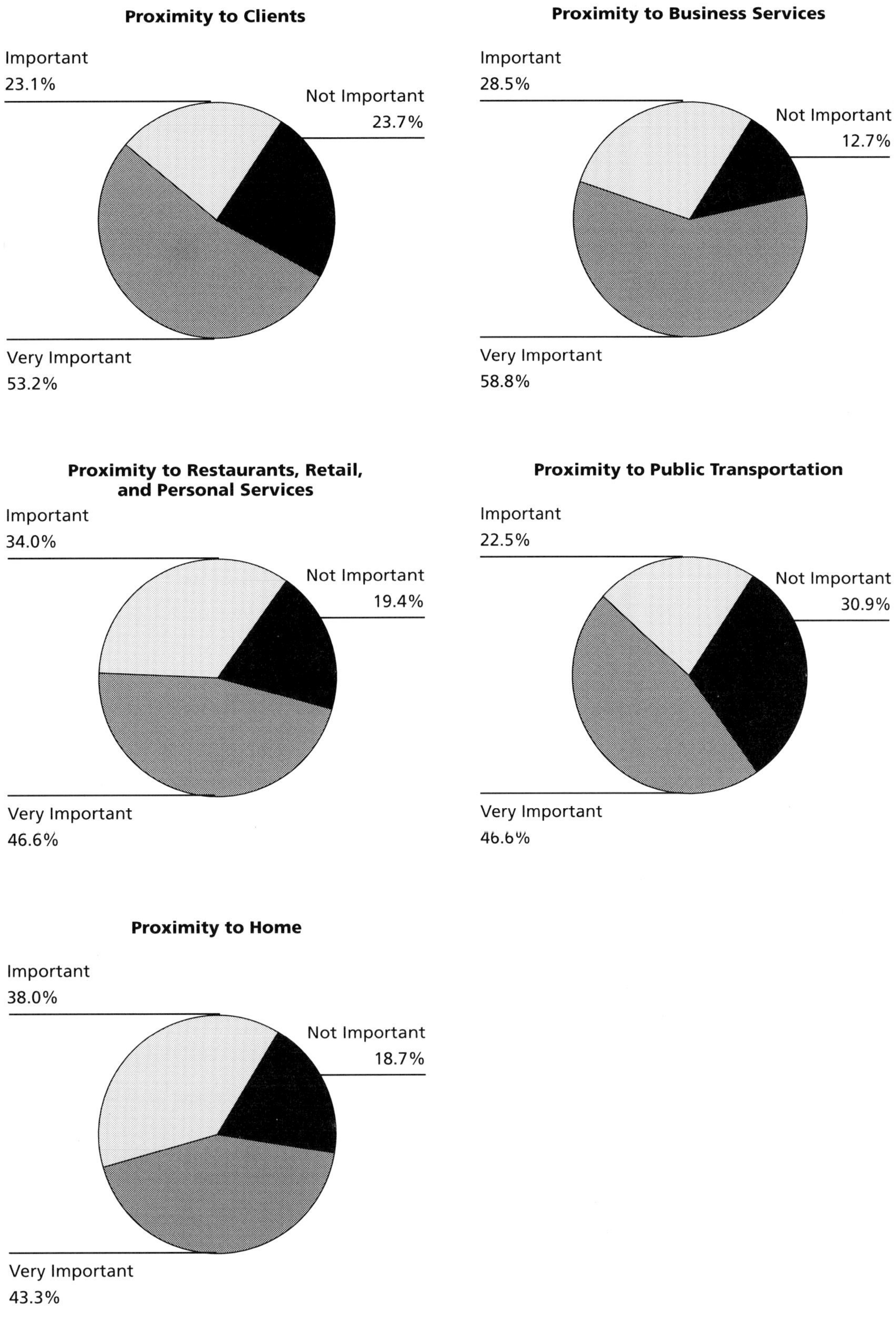

- *Proximity to restaurants/retail/personal services* is more important to tenants in real estate and consulting firms and least important to medical services.

- *Proximity to public transportation* is more important to tenants in government and nonprofit organizations than to other types of businesses. It is least important to real estate and planning/architecture firms.

- A large percentage (no less than 89 percent) of each of the largest business groups are satisfied with all their locational features.

- Proximity to public transportation is much more important to tenants in central city downtowns than to tenants in all suburban locations (including suburban downtowns).

- The concept of proximity is relative; for example, a suburban tenant's and a central city tenant's definition of "close" could be completely different, and readers should keep that caveat in mind. Proximity to where employees live is only slightly more important to tenants in suburban locations than to tenants in central city downtowns. Similarly, proximity to business services is only slightly more important to tenants in central city downtowns than to tenants in any of the suburban locations. Most tenants, regardless of location, are very satisfied with their building's ability to meet their needs for "proximity." These issues receive some of the highest satisfaction ratings in the survey.

- Features related to proximity make up the only group of features in the entire survey for which no differences occur among tenants in Class A, B, and C buildings regarding satisfaction.

- Proximity to public transportation is less important to tenants in office spaces under 20,000 square feet than to tenants in spaces over 20,000 square feet.

General Building Features

Tenants rated the relative importance to their organization of ten general building features and their satisfaction with each one (Figure 3-4). Four of the features concern expenses, two concern the availability of parking facilities, and four cover other general features tenants commonly consider:

- Rental rates (including pass-throughs and escalations)
- Operating expenses
- Tenant improvement allowance
- Cost of parking
- On-site parking
- Covered parking
- Image and prestige of the building
- Environmentally friendly building systems and materials
- Access for the disabled
- Tenant mix.

Figure 3-4 **General Building Features**

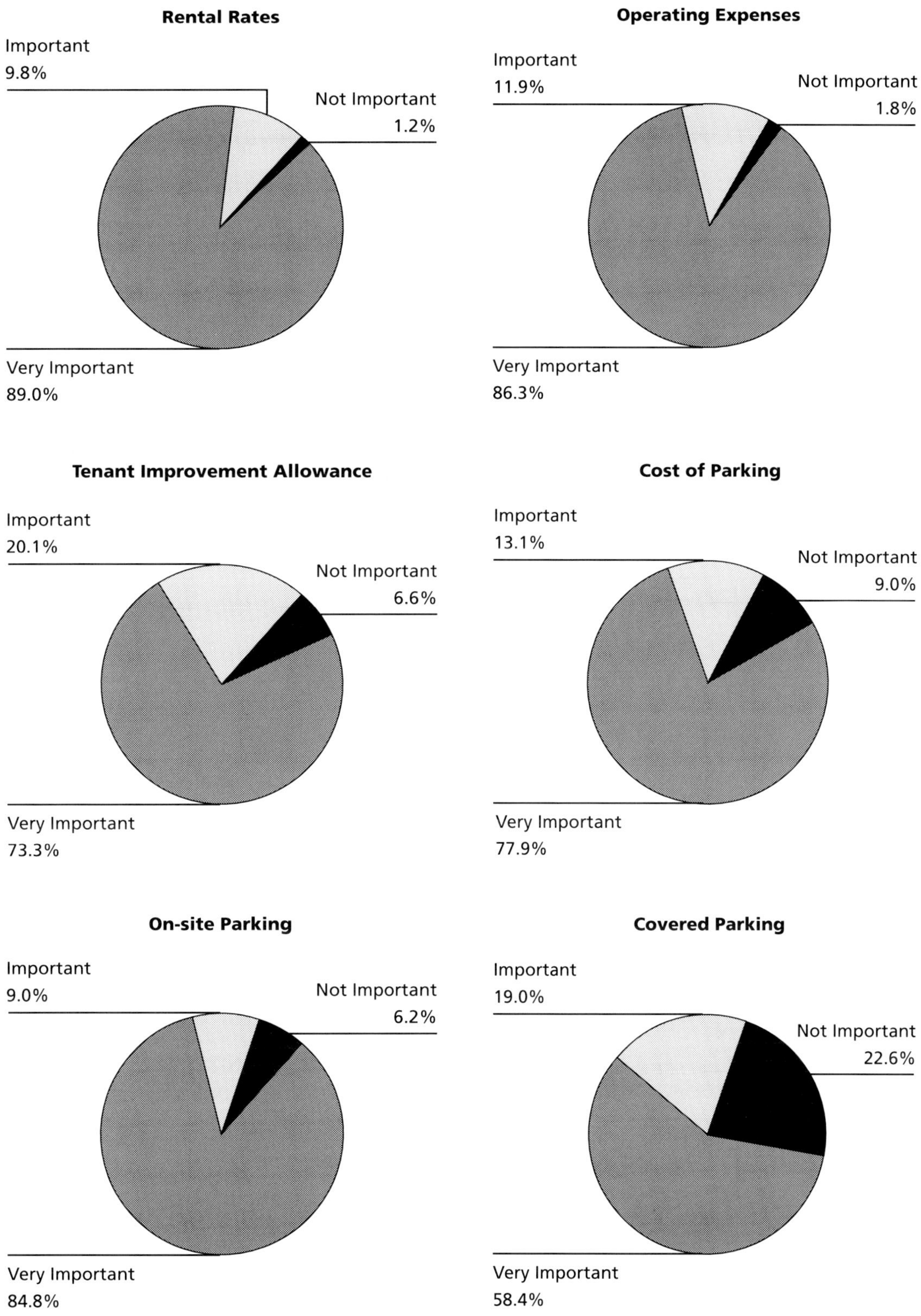

Figure 3-4 **General Building Features** (continued)

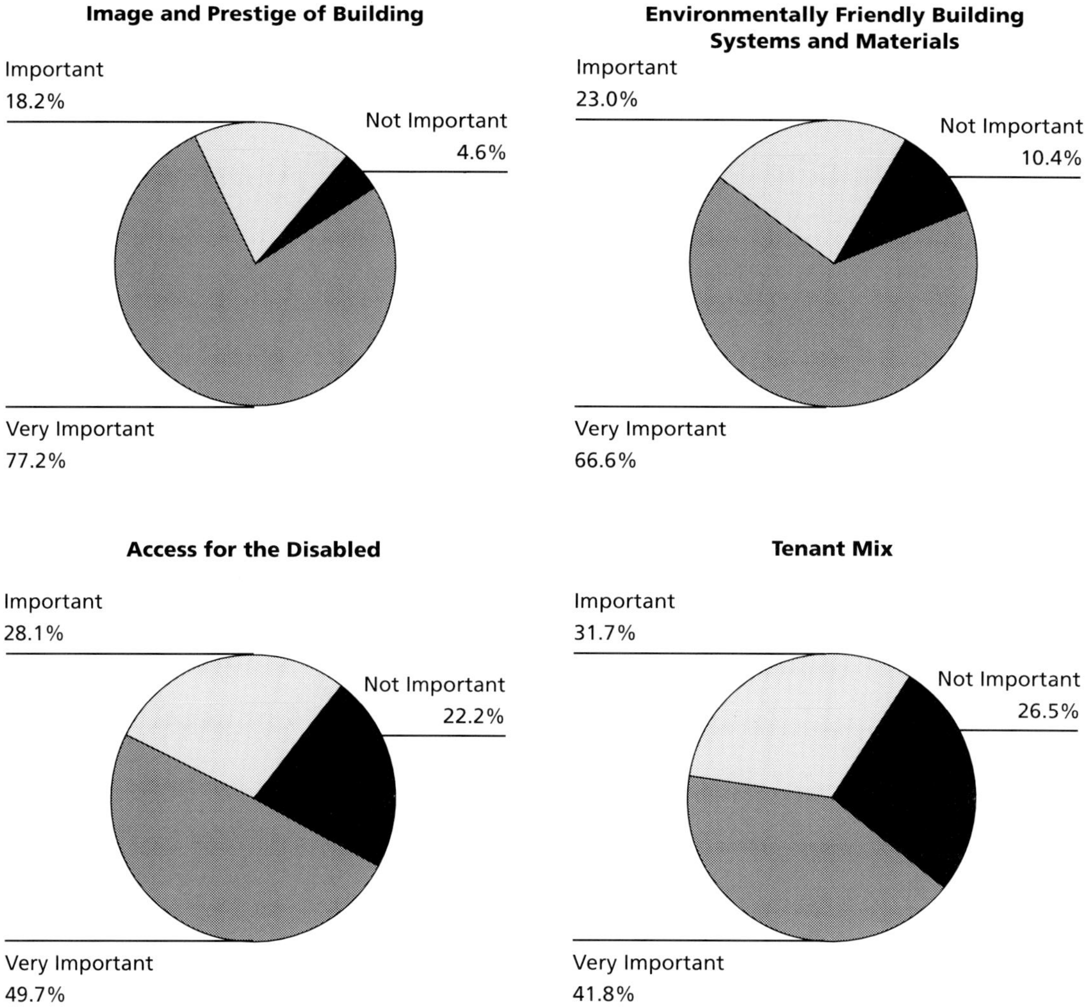

Virtually all tenants (99 percent) agree that rental rates are among the most important features considered in their evaluation of office space. Tenants rate only a handful of other features as highly in the entire survey.

The remaining general building features receive only slightly lower ratings of importance (90 to 98 percent) and also rank among the more important issues in the survey; the major exceptions are access for the disabled, rated important by 78 percent of tenants, covered parking (77 percent), and tenant mix (73 percent).

A large percentage (88 percent) of tenants for whom rental rates are important are satisfied with their current rent. At least 83 percent of tenants are in buildings that satisfy their requirements concerning all other general building features, with the exception of the three parking features.

Of the tenants for whom on-site parking, covered parking, and the cost of parking are important, only 80 percent, 77 percent, and 75 percent, respectively, are satisfied with their current arrangement. In fact, satisfaction ratings for these three parking features are among the lower satisfaction ratings in the survey.

Tenants for whom environmentally friendly building systems and materials are important accept their building's approach and generally express a high level of satisfaction (89 percent) with their current building.

Almost all tenants (92 percent) for whom access for the disabled is important indicate that their buildings meet their needs, most likely reflecting building owners' compliance with requirements mandated by the Americans with Disabilities Act.

Although tenant mix is one of the least important features in the survey, most tenants for whom the mix of tenants is important say they are in buildings that satisfy their standards. This feature has one of the highest satisfaction ratings in the survey.

- A large segment (90 percent or more) of tenants of most major business groups rate rental rates, operating expenses, tenant improvement allowance, on-site parking, building image and prestige, and cost of parking as important, with a few exceptions. Engineering firms rate the tenant improvement allowance slightly less important; accountants, planning/architecture firms, and nonprofit organizations rate on-site parking slightly less important; retailers, insurance firms, planning/architecture firms, and nonprofits rate cost of parking slightly less important; and high-tech firms rate the building's image and prestige as slightly less important.

- Covered parking, one of the lower-rated features in terms of overall importance, is most important to legal services, communications firms, consulting companies, and financial services.

- Tenant mix, also one of the lower-rated features in terms of overall importance, is rated highest by legal services, communications firms, and consulting companies.

- As might be expected, government agencies and medical services are concerned the most about access for the disabled.

* At least 80 percent of each of the largest business groups are in buildings that satisfy their expectations regarding rental rates, operating expenses, the tenant improvement allowance, the building's image and prestige, environmentally friendly building systems and materials, access for the disabled, and tenant mix. The exceptions are minor and include medical services' satisfaction with rental rates; medical services', retailers', and planning/architecture firms' satisfaction with the tenant improvement allowance in their building; and planning/architecture firms' satisfaction with access for the disabled.

* Of the three parking features, on-site parking receives the highest satisfaction ratings from government agencies, real estate firms, and engineering firms; cost of parking receives the highest ratings from real estate firms, accountants, and medical services; and covered parking receives the highest ratings from government agencies, engineering firms, legal firms, and nonprofits.

* Tenants in office parks are less concerned with covered parking than tenants in suburban and central city downtowns, but tenants in office parks for whom covered parking is important are less satisfied with their current arrangements than tenants in other locations.

* Central city tenants are the least satisfied with the cost of parking, even though little variation exists among locations in terms of importance.

* Class C tenants are slightly less satisfied with rental rates than tenants in Class A and B buildings.

* Class C building tenants are consistently far less satisfied than tenants in Class A and B buildings with many other general building features, including tenant improvement allowance, on-site parking, covered parking, access for the disabled, environmentally friendly building systems and materials, and the building's image and prestige. The lack of variation in importance by building class, coupled with the discrepancy in satisfaction, points out the variation between the rent that tenants in Class C buildings are willing to pay and the level of service they would like to receive.

Features of Building Exterior

Tenants rated the relative importance to their organization of six features of the building exterior and their satisfaction with each one (Figure 3-5). Two of the features concern exterior appearances, and four concern other exterior features tenants might consider:

* Appearance of the building
* Appearance of the grounds and landscaping
* Outside signage for the tenant's organization
* Outside loading docks
* Operable windows
* Roof-loading capacity.

Figure 3-5 **Features of Building Exterior**

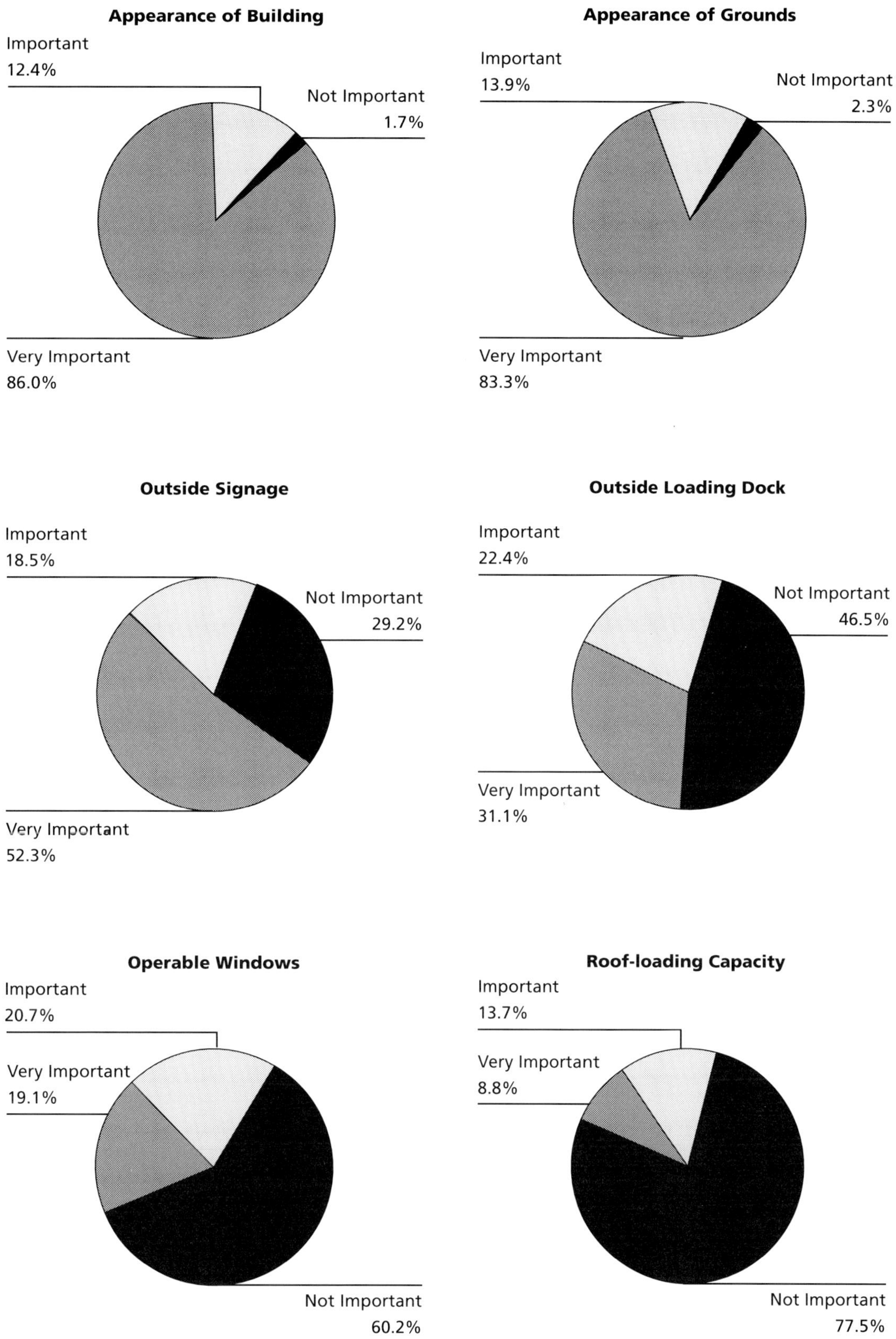

Almost all tenants (98 percent) agree that the appearance of the building and of the grounds and landscaping is important. These two features are among the more highly rated ones in the survey.

The other four exterior features—outside signage for the tenant's organization, outside loading docks, operable windows, and roof-loading capacity—are among the least important features in the survey.

At least 92 percent of respondents are in buildings that satisfy their standards with regard to the appearance of the building and grounds/landscaping, and 90 percent of the small group of tenants to whom roof-loading capacity is important are in buildings that meet their needs.

About 80 percent of respondents are in buildings that meet their needs for outside signage and outside loading docks. Only 61 percent of the tenants for whom operable windows are important are satisfied with the availability of this feature.

- Most tenants (90 percent or more) in each of the largest types of businesses rate appearance of building and appearance of grounds/landscaping as important. Most tenants (90 percent) in each business group also express satisfaction with the current exterior appearance of their building. The only exception is tenants in architecture/planning, who are slightly less satisfied with exterior appearances.

- Of the less important features, outside loading docks are more important to government agencies and communications firms than other business groups; outside signage is more important to retailers, medical services, and financial services; and operable windows are more important to nonprofits and medical services.

- Outside signage for the organization is most important to tenants in office parks.

- Although ratings of importance do not differ among tenants in Class A, B, and C buildings, tenants in Class C buildings are consistently less satisfied with five exterior building features: exterior appearance of the building, appearance of the grounds/landscaping, outside signage for their organization, outside loading docks, and roof-loading capacity.

- Three exterior features are far more important to larger tenants. Outside loading docks and roof-loading capacity are more important to firms that occupy more than 250,000 square feet than to firms that occupy less space, while outside signage is more important to firms that occupy over 100,000 square feet.

Features Of Interior Common Areas

Tenants rated the relative importance to their organization of five features of interior common areas and their satisfaction with each one (Figure 3-6). Two features describe interior appearances, two pertain to security, and one is related to elevators:

- Appearance of entry lobby (style/finishes)
- Appearance of common areas other than lobby
- Buildingwide security systems during work day
- Buildingwide security systems after hours
- Elevator service speed.

Practically all respondents (97 percent) rate the appearance of the entry lobby and other common areas, and buildingwide security systems during the work day important.

At least 84 percent of tenants are satisfied with their building in terms of security (both during and after work hours) and appearance. Elevator service speed is one of the lowest-rated features (72 percent satisfied) in the survey in terms of satisfaction.

- The vast majority (90 percent or more) of each of the largest business groups rate buildingwide security after hours, appearance of the entry lobby, and appearance of common areas other than the lobby important.

- Buildingwide security during the day is rated most important by financial and communications firms. It is the least important to real estate firms and planning/architecture firms.

- Elevator service speed is rated highest by legal and communications firms and least important by retailers and planning/architecture firms.

- At least 80 percent of respondents in most of the largest business groups are in buildings that satisfy their standards with regard to the appearance of the entry lobby and other common areas, and buildingwide security during and after hours. Two exceptions are that just under 80 percent of tenants in medical services are satisfied with buildingwide security during and after hours, and only about 70 percent of planning/architecture firms are satisfied with the appearance of the lobby and other common areas.

- As might be expected, elevator service speed is more important to tenants in central city and suburban downtowns than to tenants in other suburban locations.

- Building security during the work day is more important to respondents in central cities and suburban downtowns than in office parks and other suburban locations.

- Tenants in Class C buildings are consistently far less satisfied than tenants in Class A and B buildings with all features of interior common areas; however, ratings in importance do not differ among building types.

Figure 3-6 **Features of Interior Common Areas**

Appearance of Entry Lobby

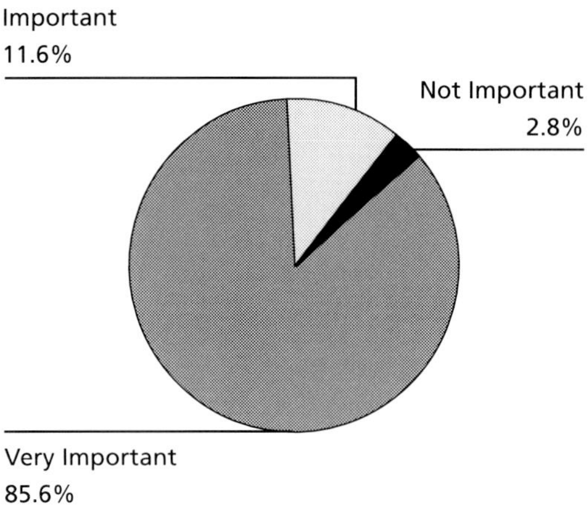

Appearance of Other Common Areas

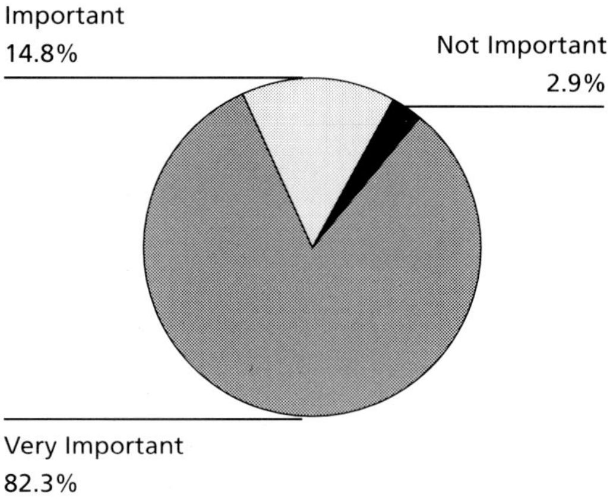

Security during Work Day

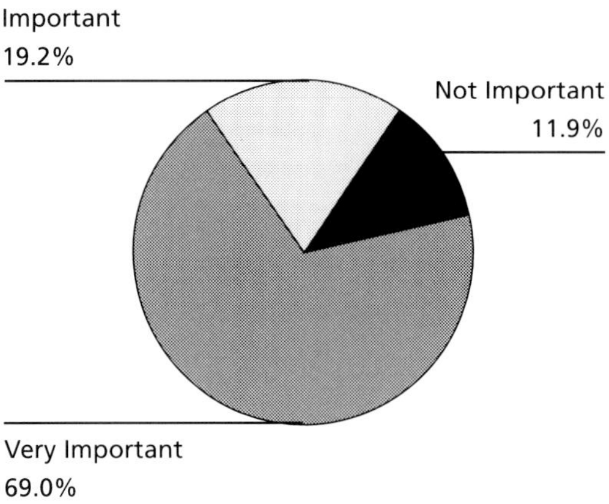

After-hours Security

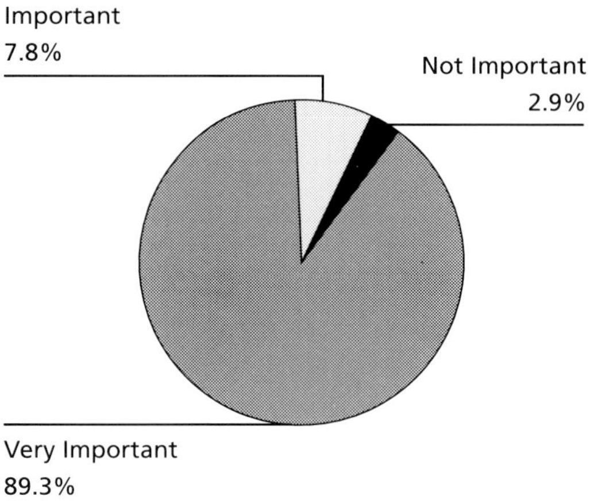

Elevator Speed

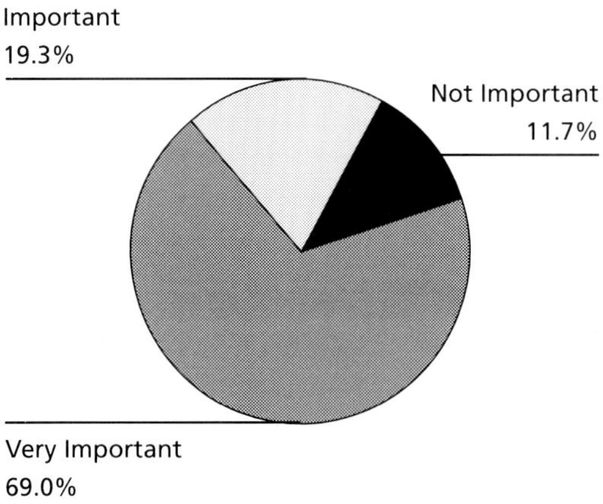

Features of Tenants' Office Suites

Tenants rated the relative importance to their organization of ten features of their office suite and their satisfaction with each one (Figure 3-7). Four features pertain to the interior environment, two describe a tenant's proximity to building facilities, and four relate to other features of an office suite tenants commonly consider:

- Indoor air quality
- Acoustics/noise control
- Comfortable temperature
- Tenant's ability to control temperature
- Proximity to elevators
- Proximity to restrooms
- Cost of after-hours heating/cooling
- Power capacity
- Security/controlled access
- Flexible suite layout (e.g., easily reconfigured).

Tenants unanimously agree (99 percent) that indoor air quality, acoustics/noise control, and comfortable temperatures are among the most important features considered in their evaluation of office space. Only a handful of other features in the survey are rated as highly.

Ninety-two to 98 percent of tenants rate a tenant's ability to control temperature, proximity to restrooms, power capacity, security/controlled access, and a flexible suite layout important.

At least 80 percent of tenants are satisfied that their building provides all but two of the features related to office suites. Not surprisingly, office temperature and a tenant's ability to control temperature do not meet respondents' expectations as much as other features do. These two features are among the lowest-rated features in the survey in terms of satisfaction.

Almost all (98 percent) of respondents are satisfied with their proximity to elevators, even though it is the least important feature of office suites. In fact, proximity to elevators receives one of the three highest satisfaction ratings in the survey.

- A large segment (90 percent or more) of tenants in most of the major business groups rate indoor air quality, acoustics/noise control, proximity to restrooms, power capacity, comfortable temperature, tenant's ability to control temperature, security/controlled access, and flexible suite layout important.

Figure 3-7 **Features of Tenants' Office Suites**

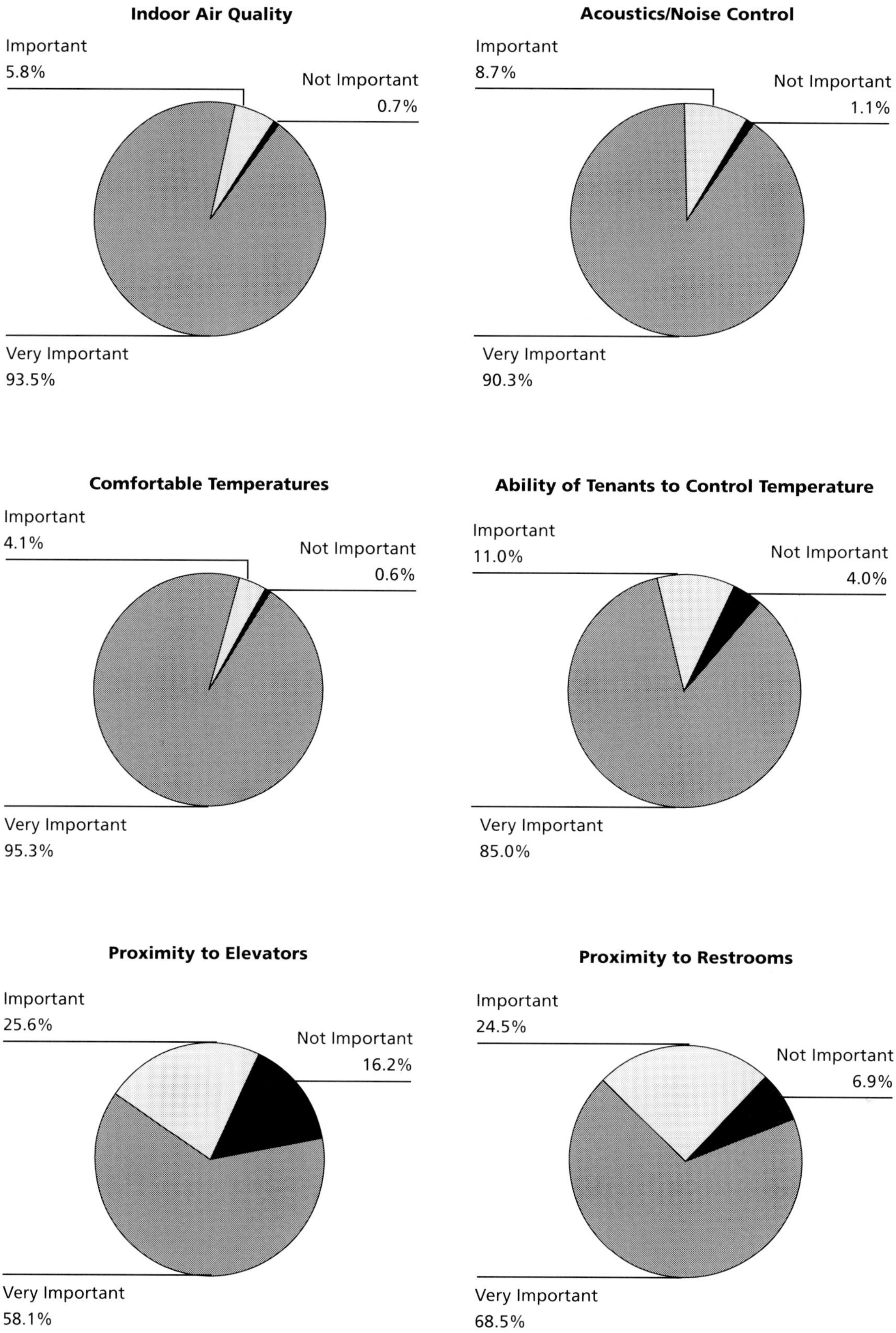

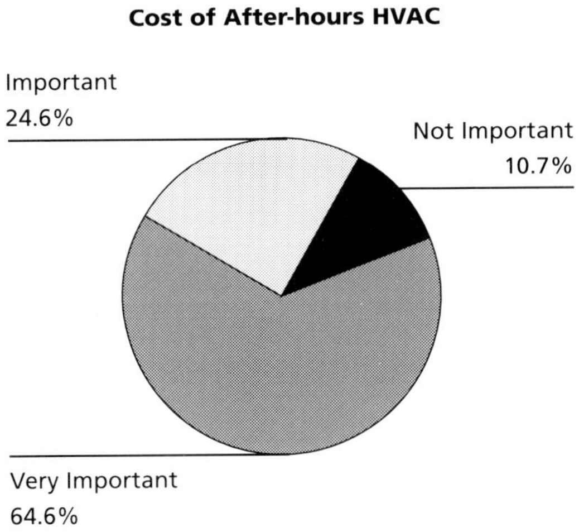

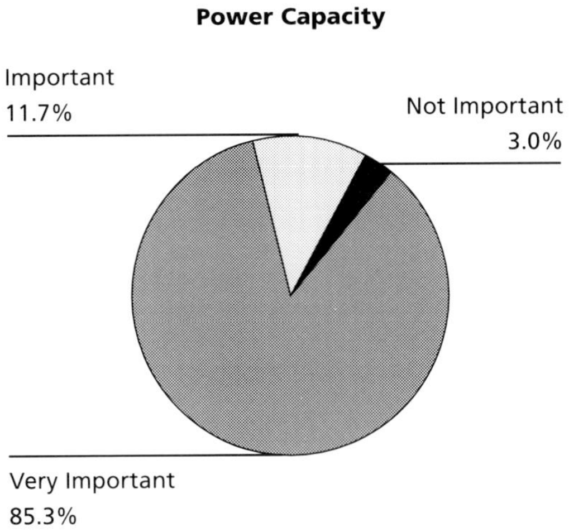

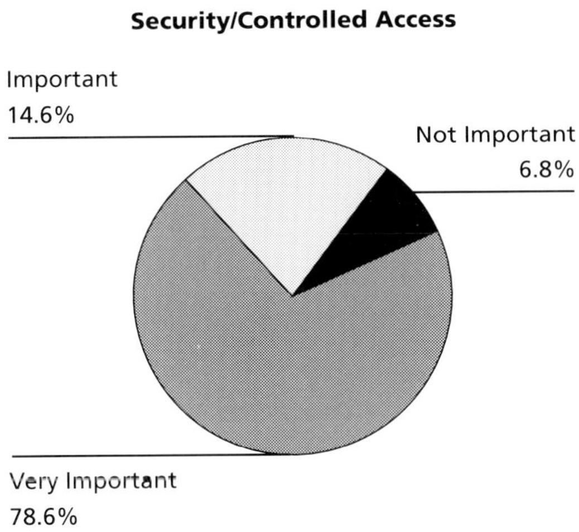

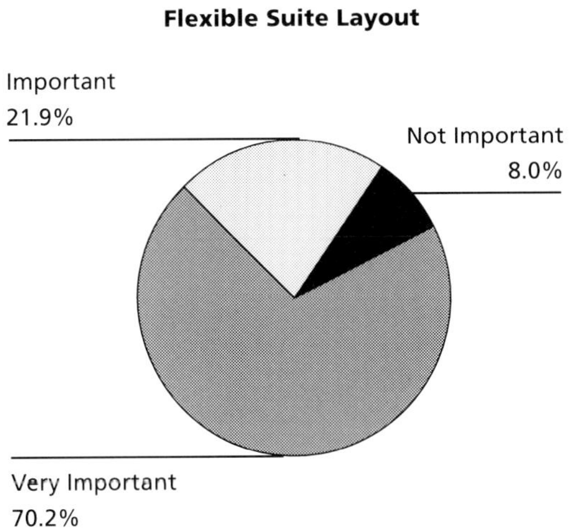

- Some exceptions are apparent, however, for three of these features. Proximity to restrooms is less important to retailers and real estate firms; security/controlled access is less important to retailers, real estate firms, and planning/architecture firms; and flexible suite layout is less important to retailers, nonprofits, legal services, and accounting firms.

- Proximity to elevators is rated most highly by legal services, government agencies, medical services, and financial services. Retailers, real estate firms, and planning/architecture firms rate it least important.

- Cost of after-hours heating/cooling is rated most important by engineering, high-tech, and medical service firms, and lowest by real estate firms and retailers.

- At least 80 percent of the largest business groups are in buildings that satisfy their requirements for indoor air quality, acoustics/noise control, power capacity, proximity to elevators, proximity to restrooms, security/controlled access, and flexible suite layout. Exceptions include high-tech firms, legal services, communications firms, and medical services, which are slightly less satisfied with indoor air quality, and legal services, nonprofits, accountants, planning/architecture firms, consulting firms, and medical services, which are slightly less satisfied with acoustics and noise control.

- Comfortable temperature, one the lowest-rated features overall in the survey in terms of satisfaction (74 percent), receives the highest satisfaction ratings from engineering, insurance, and financial service firms, and government agencies, most of which occupy the larger spaces.

- A tenant's ability to control temperature, also one of the lowest-rated features overall in terms of satisfaction (65 percent), receives the highest satisfaction ratings from communications firms and planning/architecture firms.

- The cost of after-hours heating/cooling, which 79 percent of respondents overall are satisfied with, receives the highest satisfaction ratings from real estate firms, government agencies, and financial services.

- Tenants in Class C buildings are far less satisfied than tenants in Class A and B buildings with four features of office suites: indoor air quality, acoustics/noise control, comfortable temperature, and the tenant's ability to control temperature. Still, ratings in importance do not differ among tenants in Class A, B, and C buildings.

- Even though ratings in importance do not differ by size of tenant, tenants in the largest office spaces (generally 100,000 square feet and more) are more satisfied than tenants in the smallest spaces (generally 10,000 square feet or less) with indoor air quality, acoustics/noise control, comfortable temperature, and the tenant's ability to control temperature.

Building Amenities and Services

Tenants rated the relative importance to their organization of nine building amenities and services and their satisfaction with each one (Figure 3-8). Four of the features concern the availability of personal amenities, three concern the availability of shared business services/facilities, and two are other features that can be found in office buildings:

- Food service
- Convenience retail stores
- Fitness center
- Child-care facility
- Shared videoconference facility
- Shared teleconference facility
- Shared business services (e.g., data and word processing)
- Concierge
- Banking/ATM.

Building amenities are among the least important of all features in the survey and, as a group, show a wide variation in level of importance to tenants: 75 percent of respondents rate food service important, but only 29 percent rate shared business services important. Readers must note, however, that for those who do rate them as important, building amenities are among the lowest-rated features in terms of satisfaction.

Shared conferencing facilities, fitness centers, and child-care facilities receive thc lowest satisfaction ratings in the entire survey. Only about 60 percent of respondents to whom fitness centers and conferencing facilities are important are currently satisfied with the facilities in their building, and just under 50 percent of respondents to whom child-care facilities are important are now satisfied with the availability of facilities in or near their building.

Nevertheless, while availability of a concierge and shared business services are important to a relatively small group of tenants, many respondents have been able to find a building that satisfactorily offers these amenities.

Many tenants are satisfied with the availability of food service, banking/ATM facilities, and convenience retail stores in their building; between 71 and 81 percent indicate that the current availability of these amenities meets their requirements.

- The availability of child-care facilities is more important to tenants in government agencies, and to high-tech and insurance firms.

Figure 3-8 **Building Amenities and Services**

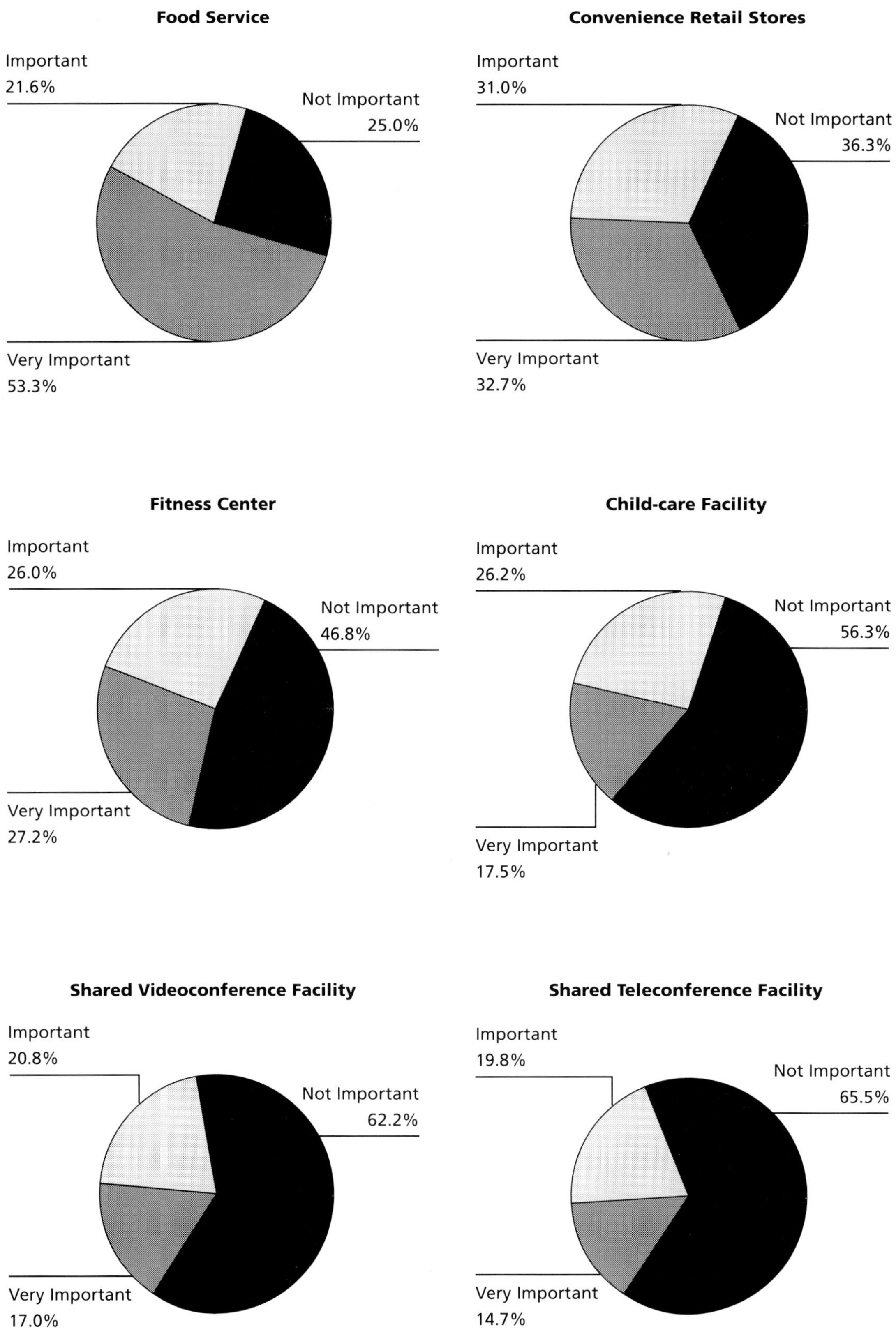

Shared Business Services

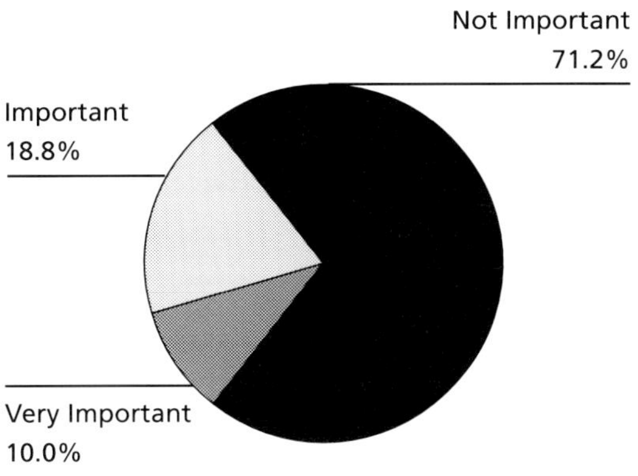

Concierge

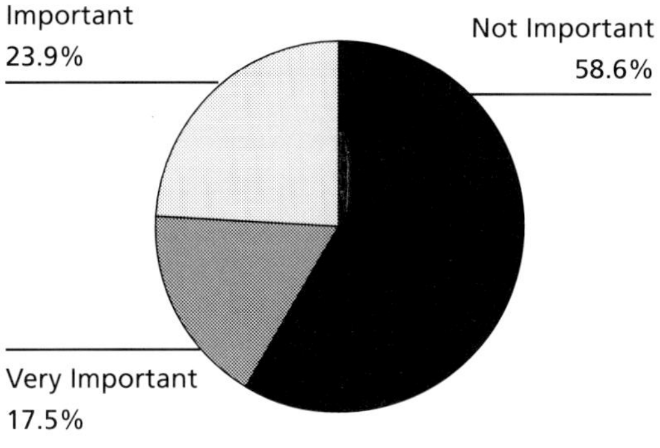

Banking/ATM

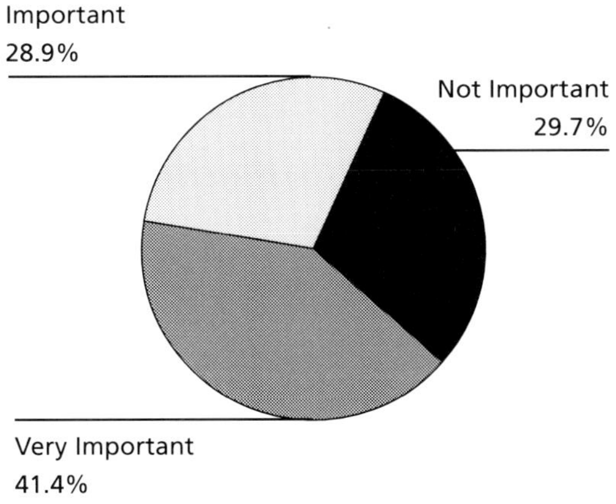

- The availability of food service is more important to tenants in government agencies and financial services.

- Engineering firms are the most interested in shared videoconferencing and teleconferencing facilities.

- Planning/architecture firms are the least interested of all business types in many of the building amenities, including banking/ATM, child-care facilities, availability of a concierge, fitness center, food service, and convenience stores.

- Even though ratings of importance do not differ among tenants in Class A, B, and C buildings, tenants in Class C buildings are consistently less satisfied than tenants in Class A and B buildings with almost all building amenities.

- The largest tenants, those with 250,000 square feet or more, are more interested than smaller tenants (primarily those with 10,000 square feet or less) in banking/ATM, child-care facilities, fitness centers, food service, and conferencing facilities.

Building Management

Tenants rated the relative importance to their organization of six features of building management and their satisfaction with each one (Figure 3-9). Two of the features concern the availability of on-site personnel, and four describe the building staff's performance:

- On-site building management staff
- On-site security guard
- Building management's responsiveness
- Building management's ability to meet tenants' needs
- Effectiveness of communications with building management
- Quality of building maintenance work.

Virtually all respondents (99 percent) agree that the four features pertaining to the management staff's performance are important in their evaluation of office space. Only one general building feature and three features of office suites are as highly rated.

A slightly lower percentage of tenants (about 90 percent) rate features concerning on-site personnel important.

Most tenants are located in office buildings that meet their expectations regarding building management. Over 85 percent of respondents are satisfied with the current building management's performance and the availability of on-site personnel.

- A large segment (90 percent or more) of tenants in the major business groups rate features of the building's management important, although two of the features are slightly less important to certain businesses. Planning/architecture, real estate, engineering, and retailing rate an on-site staff slightly below the norm, and real estate, high-tech, engineering, and retailing firms rate the availability of an on-site security guard lower than others. Only 64 percent of planning/architecture firms assign importance to on-site security guards.

Figure 3-9 Building Management

On-site Staff

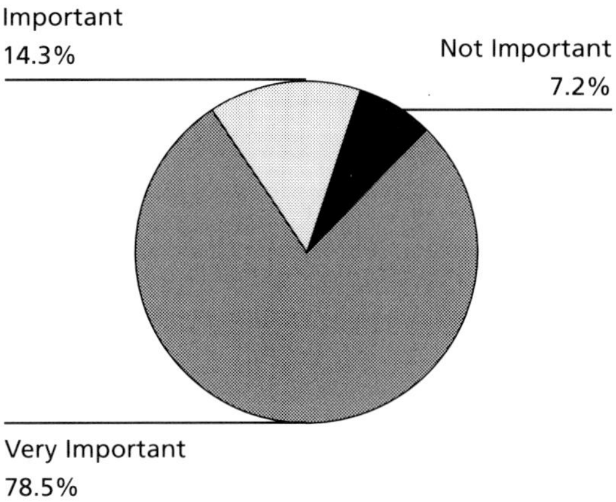

On-site Security Guard

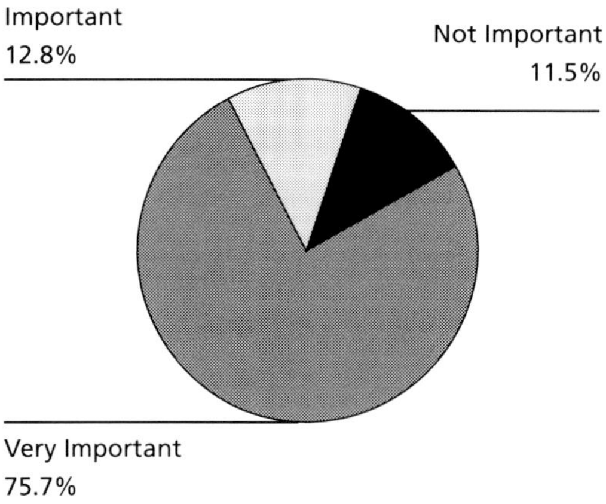

Responsiveness of Staff

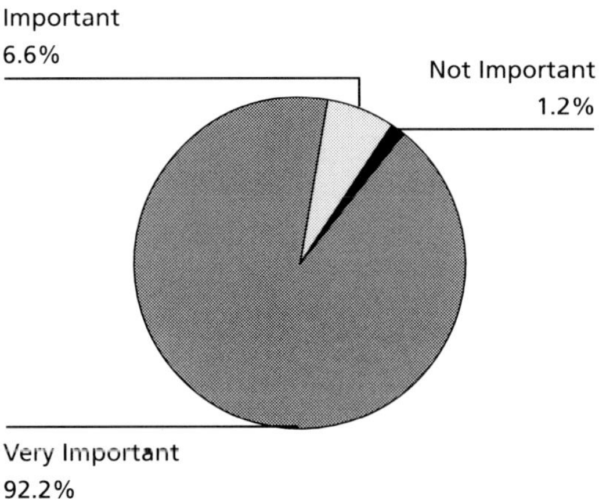

Ability of Staff to Meet Tenants' Needs

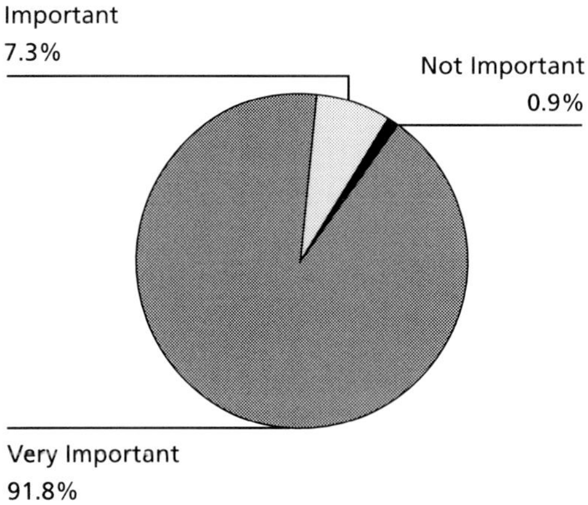

Effectiveness of Communications with Management

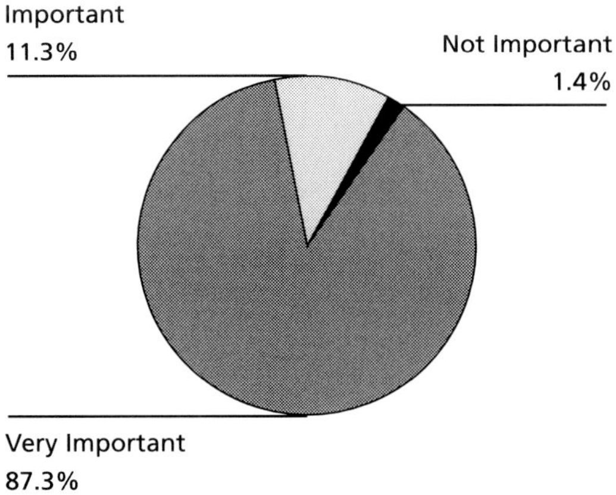

Quality of Maintenance Work

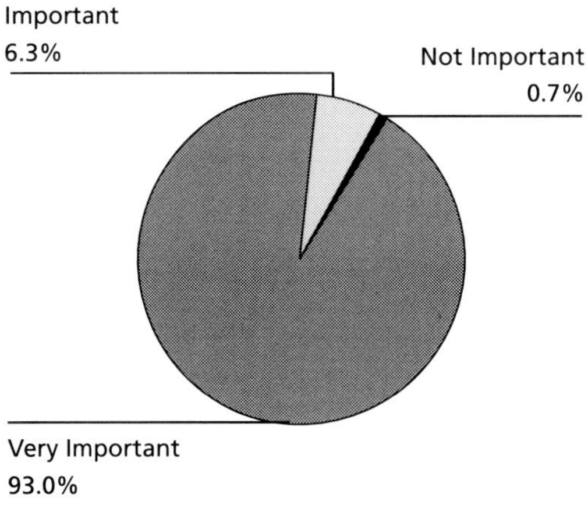

- As might be expected, tenants in both central city and suburban downtowns rate on-site security guards more important than tenants in office parks and other suburban locations. Still, a large majority of tenants in all locations say that an on-site security guard is important.

- At least 80 percent of the largest business groups are satisfied with each feature pertaining to the building's management. The exceptions are minor and include business groups where just under 80 percent of tenants are satisfied with features: planning/architecture firms' satisfaction with the effectiveness of communications with management, and planning/architecture firms', engineering firms', and medical services' satisfaction with the availability of on-site security guards.

- Tenants in Class C buildings are consistently far less satisfied than tenants in Class A and B buildings with all features of building management. Yet Class C tenants do not differ from Class A and B tenants in their ratings of importance of most building management features.

4

Intelligent Building Features

Tenants were asked to review a list of 13 intelligent building systems and structural features and indicate which ones are currently available in their building (Figure 4-1). Eight features involve support of tenants' computer and/or communications functions; the other five relate to general building functions:

- Fiber-optics capability
- Built-in wiring for Internet access
- Wiring for high-speed networks
- LAN and WAN connectivity
- Satellite accessibility
- ISDN
- Redundant power source
- Conduits for power/data/voice cabling
- High-tech, energy-efficient HVAC system
- Automatic on/off sensor in the lighting system
- "Smart" elevators that group passengers by floor designation
- Automatic sensors installed in faucets/toilets
- Computerized/interactive building directory.

Tenants were then asked to rank the three features that are most important to their organization, to specify any features that their organization needs but are not currently available in their building, and to indicate whether they would be willing to pay additional rent to have those features.

Only 56 percent of all respondents are located in buildings with any of the intelligent features listed in the survey. Features involving computer/communications functions are the most commonly available, with built-in wiring for access to the Internet the most prevalent feature, found in almost 25 percent of tenants' buildings.

General building functions are less common and are found in no more than 12 percent of buildings, with one exception. High-tech, energy-efficient HVAC systems are found in 23 percent of tenants' buildings.

In tenants' rating of the importance of intelligent building features to their business, no single intelligent building feature stands out, but six features are consistently among tenants' top three: HVAC systems, wiring for Internet access, wiring for high-speed networks, LAN/WAN connectivity, fiber-optics capability, and conduits for power/data/voice cabling.

Photo credit for page 41
Coopers & Lybrand
Embankment Place
London, England
Reproduced with permission from *Corporate Interiors No. 1*
Design Firm: Swanke Hayden Connell Architects
Photography: Jeremy Cockayne

Figure 4-1 **Intelligent Building Features**

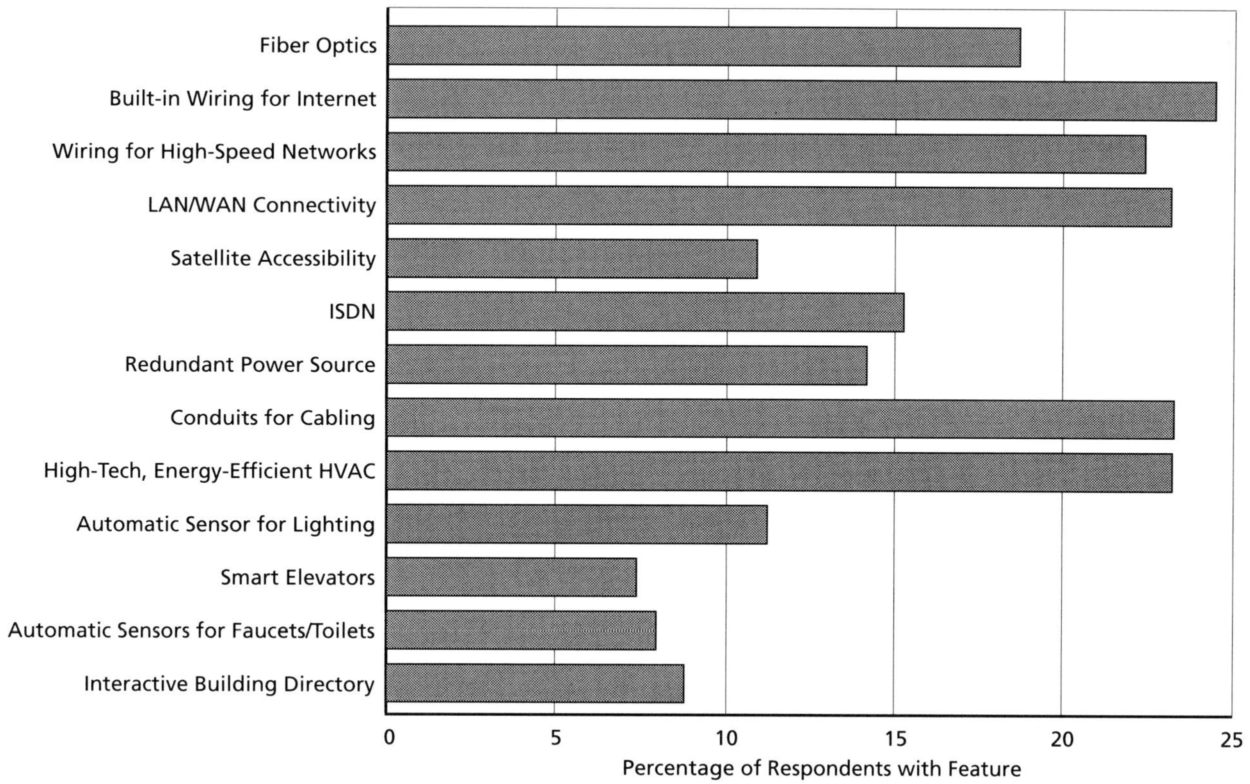

The relatively high ranking of HVAC systems in this list corroborates the importance tenants place on having a comfortable temperature in their office and having control over the office temperature.

Tenants were also asked to mention any intelligent building features their organization needs but are not available in their building. Only 11 percent of respondents mentioned any other features; the most commonly desired features are telecommunications capability (cable TV access, fiber-optics capability, videoconferencing, satellite access), computer-related features (wiring for Internet access, wiring for high-speed networks), HVAC system (energy efficient, ability to control the temperature in their own suite), security system (camera/monitoring, controlled access), and a redundant power source.

Many respondents (72 percent) are willing to pay additional rent to have the features made available (although very few specify the extra amount they would be willing to pay). When money is attached, however, the priority of features changes. The top five features respondents are willing to pay for, in order, are computer-related features, HVAC system, security system, telecommunications capability, and a redundant power source.

A higher proportion of tenants in insurance, high-tech businesses, and government have chosen buildings with intelligent building features (Figure 4-2). (Some business groups, such as utilities, are not included in this analysis because the sample of respondents was too small.) Although some portion of virtually all the business groups are located in intelligent buildings, the groups that have the lowest proportion in such buildings are retailers, medical services, legal services, consulting firms, and accounting firms:

- Financial services, insurance, high-tech firms, and government agencies have more often located in a building with LAN and WAN connectivity.

- Buildings with built-in wiring for Internet access and high-speed networks are most appealing to insurance firms, high-tech firms, and government agencies (about 39 percent).

- Buildings with conduits for power/data/voice cabling are most appealing to financial services, insurance, and government agencies.

- Thirty-three percent of tenants in insurance and government, and about 22 percent of financial, real estate, and high-tech firms have chosen buildings with fiber-optics capability.

- About 30 percent of tenants in financial services, insurance, and real estate, and nonprofit organizations are located in buildings that have high-tech, energy-efficient HVAC systems.

- The availability of ISDN (high-speed telephone connections) is most important to high-tech firms (30 percent). Sixteen to 23 percent of most other of the largest business groups have chosen a building with this feature. The exceptions are accountants, engineers, legal services, medical services, and retailers.

- About 23 percent of tenants in financial services, insurance, and high technology are located in buildings with a redundant power source.

- Twenty percent of tenants in financial services and insurance have chosen buildings with satellite access, and no more than 14 percent of all the other largest business groups are located in buildings with this feature.

Figure 4-2 **Use of Intelligent Building Features, by Business Group**

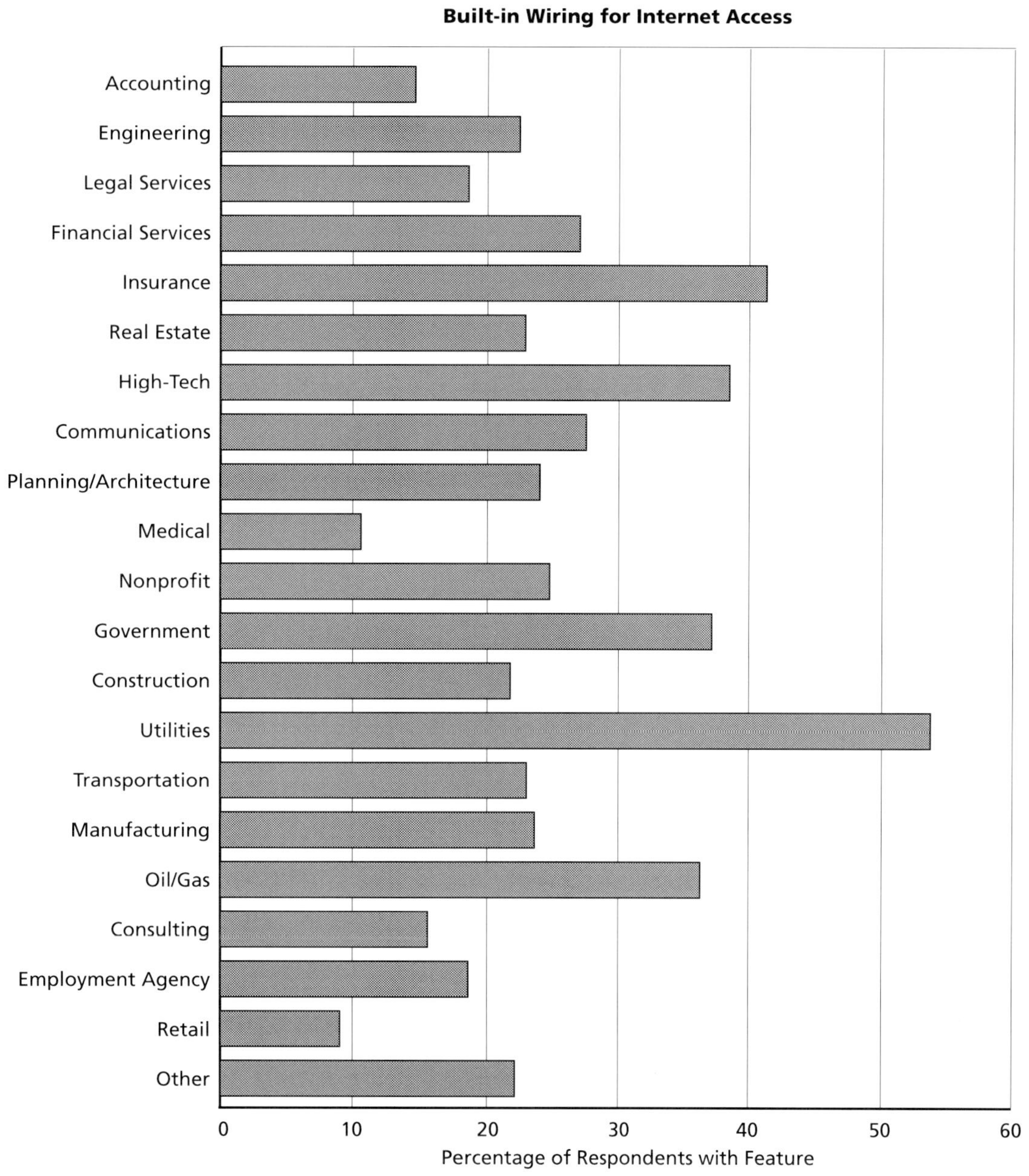

Note: Sample size for utilities and oil/gas companies was too small for meaningful analysis.

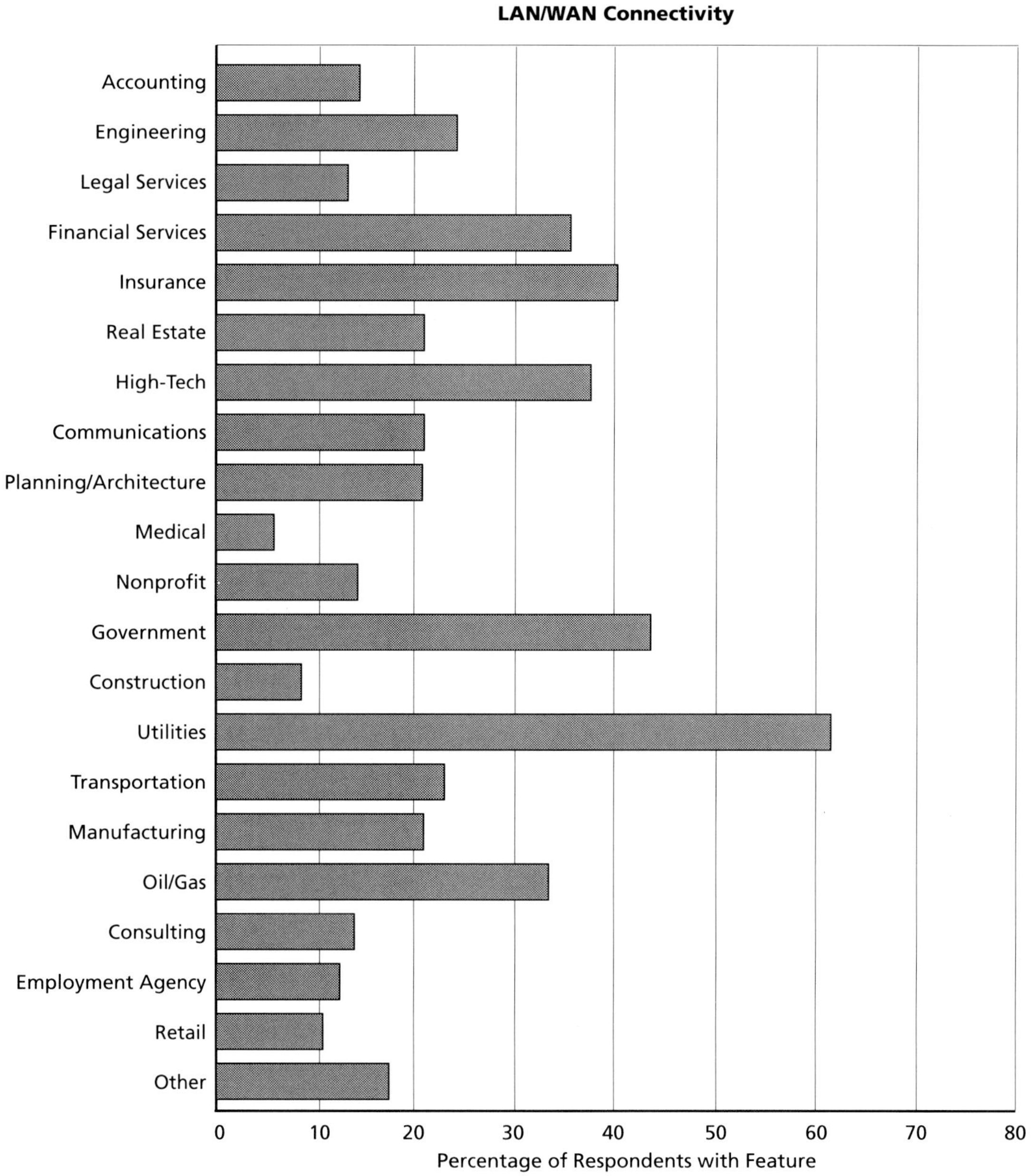

Note: Sample size for utilities and oil/gas companies was too small for meaningful analysis.

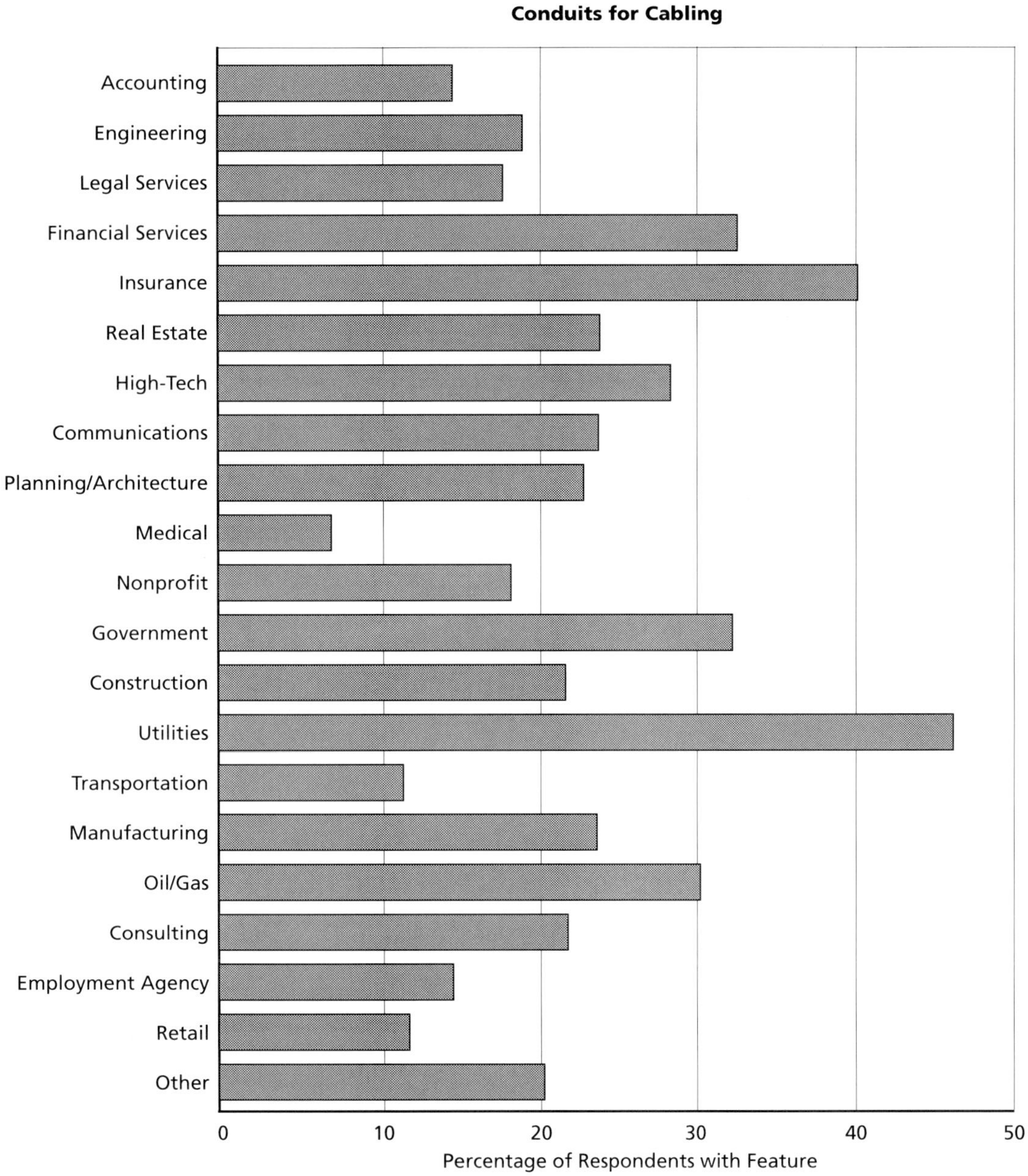

Note: Sample size for utilities and oil/gas companies was too small for meaningful analysis.

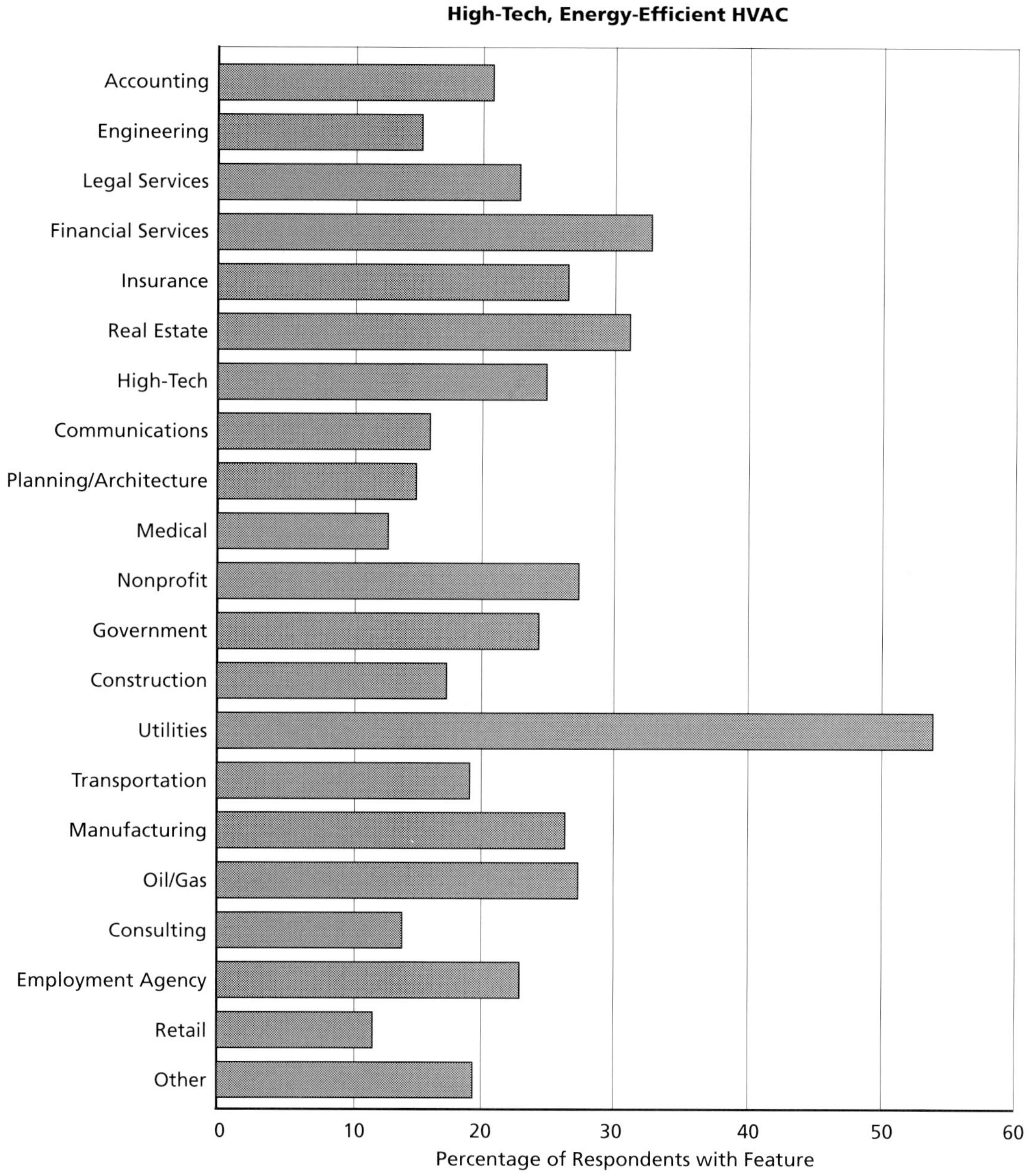

Note: Sample size for utilities and oil/gas companies was too small for meaningful analysis.

Figure 4-3 **Built-in Wiring for High-Speed Networks**

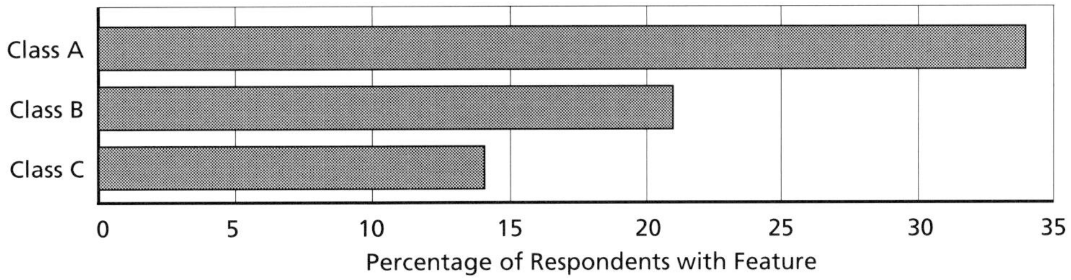

In general, tenants who want and/or need intelligent building features will find a building that offers them. For example, 39 percent of high-tech firms are located in buildings with built-in wiring for Internet access, and 42 percent rank this feature among the three most important intelligent features.

Just because an intelligent building feature is available, however, does not mean tenants will value it as important. For example, relatively fewer financial service and insurance firms and government agencies rank conduits for power/data/voice cabling among the three most important features than are in buildings with this feature, suggesting that *building owners and managers need to be careful before retrofitting their buildings with any intelligent building feature to make sure their tenants really want or need it.*

Many of the business groups with a relatively low number of tenants in buildings with built-in wiring for Internet access, wiring for high-speed networks, fiber-optics capability, or high-tech, energy-efficient HVAC systems rank these features among their most wanted intelligent features. Therefore, *these features should be the first considerations when updating a building to include intelligent building features* (Figure 4-3).

Far more of the largest tenants (in terms of numbers of employees and square footage of office space) are located in buildings with intelligent features. In fact, a fairly consistent pattern emerges in the responses concerning all intelligent features listed in the survey; that is, size of tenant and availability of intelligent building features are directly related.

The correlation is most prevalent in computer and communications support features. It is much narrower for general building functions because of the relatively low number of respondents' buildings that have these features. The exception is high-tech, energy-efficient HVAC systems: 16 percent of the smallest tenants but over 60 percent of the largest ones are located in buildings with this feature.

The correlation is most prevalent in computer and communications support features. It is much narrower for general building functions because of the relatively low number of respondents' buildings that have these features. The exception is high-tech, energy-efficient HVAC systems: 16 percent of the smallest tenants but over 60 percent of the largest ones are located in buildings with this feature.

- In a consistent pattern that does not vary by feature listed in the survey, the proportion of tenants in buildings with an intelligent building feature increases from Class C to Class B to Class A buildings.

Intelligent building features are much more prevalent in owner-occupied buildings. For example, about 50 percent of tenants who own their space have LAN and WAN connectivity, fiber-optics capability, built-in wiring for Internet access, conduits for power/data/voice cabling, wiring for high-speed networks, and high-tech, energy-efficient HVAC systems. No more than 23 percent of all lessees have any of these features in their buildings.

5

Alternative Office Strategies

Tenants were asked to indicate which, if any, of three alternative office strategies—hoteling (reserving desk space), telecommuting (in which employees can regularly work at home during normal business hours), and virtual office (the ability to conduct work in nontraditional settings)—their company uses.

They were then asked about the percentage of employees participating in these programs and to rank the top three reasons that each strategy had been implemented. Finally, they were asked about the impact of alternative office strategies on the amount of office space required by the organization and the configuration of the space.

Thirty-three percent of tenants have implemented some type of alternative office strategy. Telecommuting is the most popular alternative strategy, with 24 percent of respondents using it. Eighteen percent of respondents use virtual office, while only 7 percent of respondents use hoteling.

The use of telecommuting and virtual office facilities appears related, as 60 percent of respondents that use telecommuting also use virtual offices. In fact, it is likely that some respondents use the terms interchangeably to refer to the general practice of enabling employees to work outside the office.

The employee participation rate among companies using an alternative office strategy varies greatly from company to company (< 5 to 90 percent). For tenants that use telecommuting or hoteling, 5 to 10 percent of employees use the strategies. For those using virtual offices, the percentage is slightly higher, 10 to 20 percent.

By far the most popular reasons companies implement telecommuting are in response to demand from employees and to increase operating efficiency (Figure 5-1). About 60 percent of respondents that use telecommuting note both these reasons among their top three.

Virtual offices are implemented primarily as a means to increase operating efficiency, noted by 73 percent of respondents that use virtual offices. Unique to this format, 18 percent of companies note their use of virtual offices is in response to demand from clients.

Respondents implement hoteling to increase operating efficiency and to reduce the amount of office space needed, reasons noted by about 67 percent of companies that use hoteling.

Photo credit for page 51
Offices of Togawa & Smith, Inc.
Pasadena, California

Figure 5-1 **Reasons for Adopting Alternative Office Strategies**

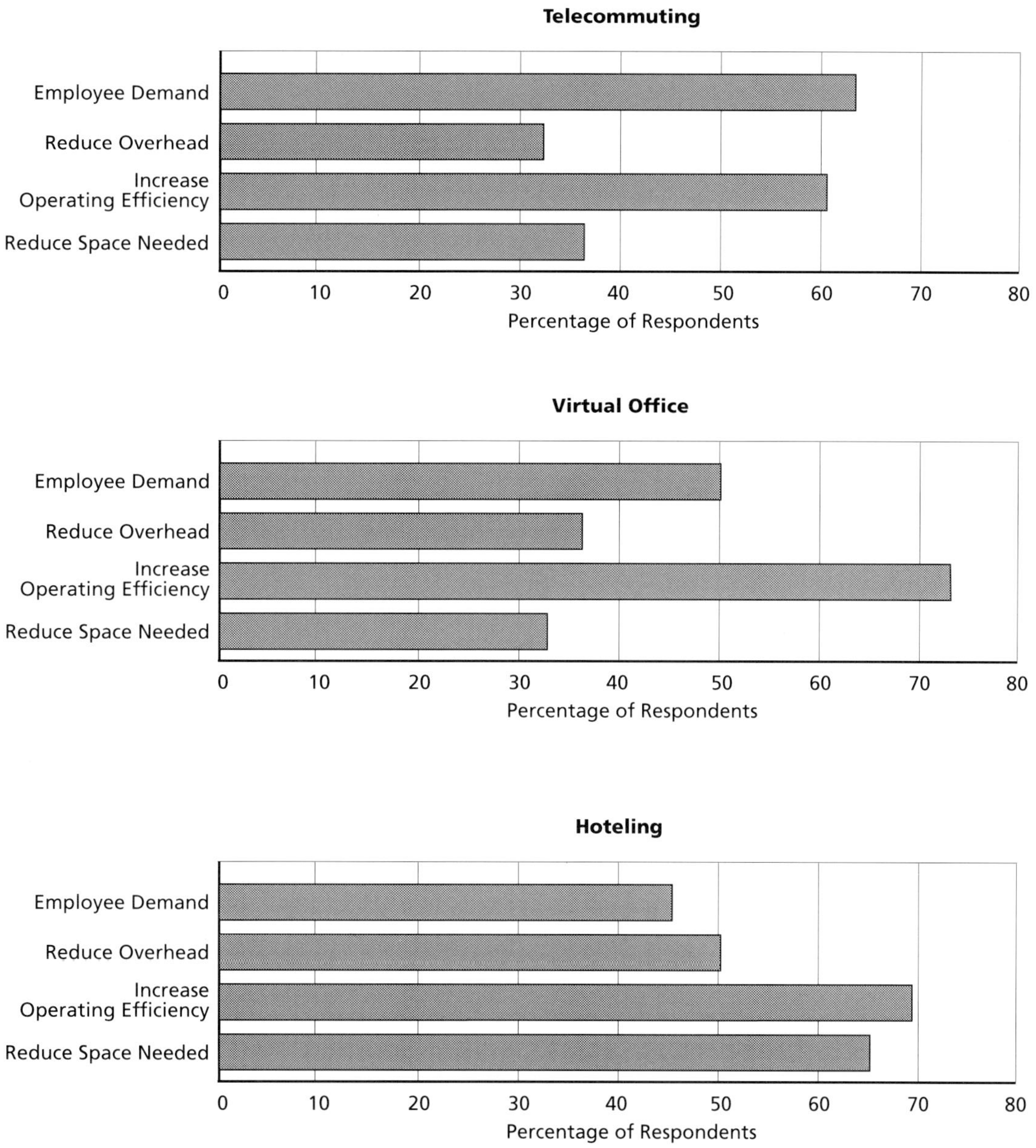

Telecommuting and virtual offices have not made a major difference in tenants' need for space (Figure 5-2). About three-quarters of companies that use telecommuting or virtual offices report that these strategies have not affected the amount of space they require. Twenty-two percent of respondents indicate a reduction in space needed (split 8 percent with a reduction of 10 percent or less and 14 percent with a reduction greater than 10 percent), while about 4 percent actually required more space.

Hoteling had a much greater effect on the amount of space needed. Only 56 percent of respondents report no change in space needed. Twenty-one percent of tenants who have adopted hoteling have needed over 10 percent less space, and 17 percent have needed 10 percent or less space. Seven percent actually required more space.

In general, the allocation of space changed little with the adoption of alternative office strategies, following about the same pattern as changing needs for space. For the 20 to 30 percent of respondents who experienced a change, the most common changes included:

- Greater use of telecommunications technology (28 percent)
- Fewer private offices (22 percent)
- More open-plan work stations (21 percent)
- More modular furniture systems (20 percent)
- More shared areas for project teams (19 percent)
- More flexible office space (18 percent)
- Less parking (6 percent).

Each strategy has a slightly different effect on the allocation of space (Figure 5-3), but in general, telecommuting and virtual offices have about the same effects as the list above. Hoteling has a greater and very different effect on the allocation of space:

- Fewer private offices (42 percent)
- More open-plan work stations (41 percent)
- More shared areas for project teams (36 percent)
- More modular furniture systems (34 percent)
- Greater use of telecommunications technology (33 percent)
- More flexible office space (26 percent)
- Less parking (7 percent).

Figure 5-2 **Impact of Alternative Office Strategies on Space Needed**

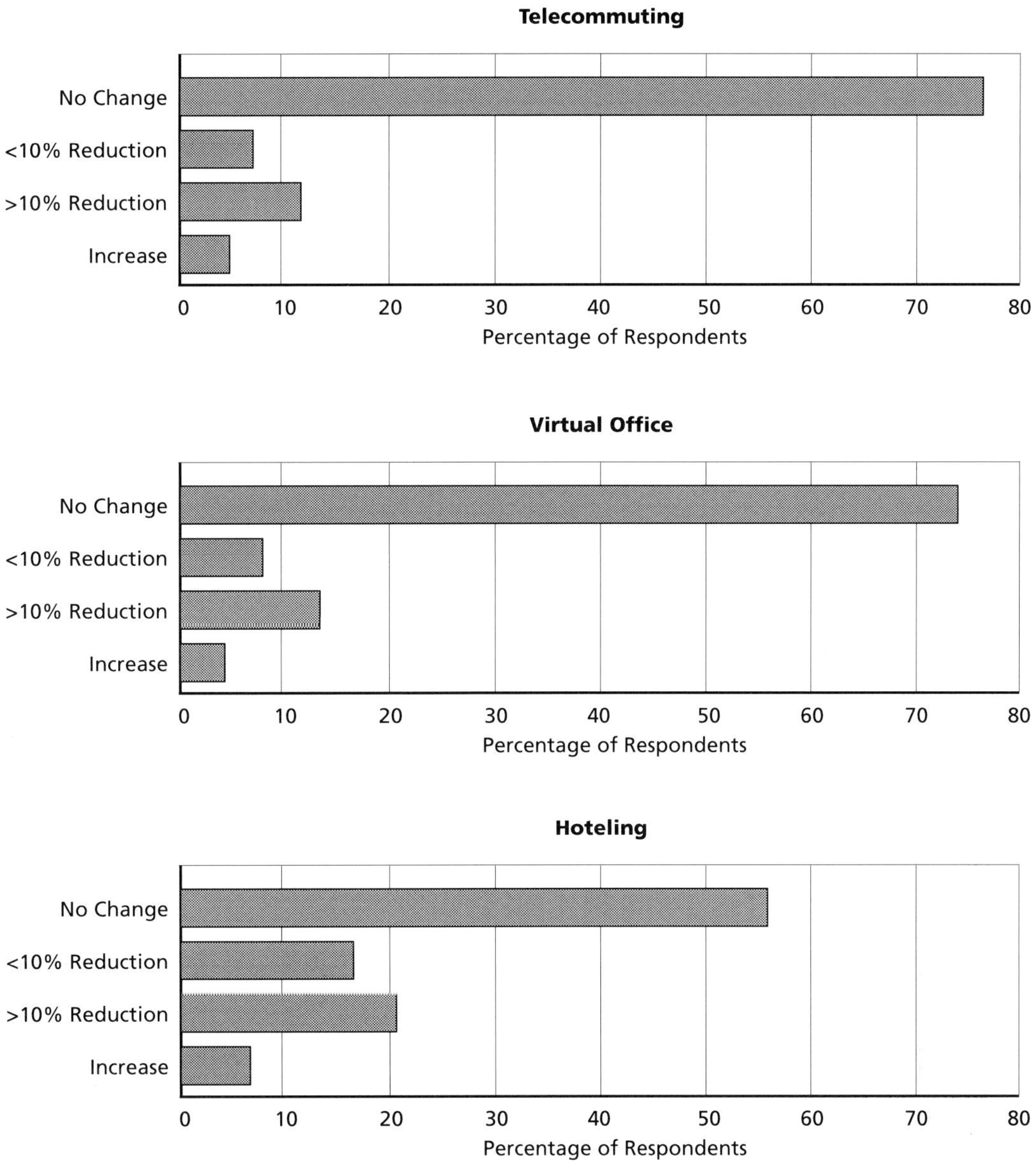

Figure 5-3 **Impact of Alternative Office Strategies on Allocation of Space**

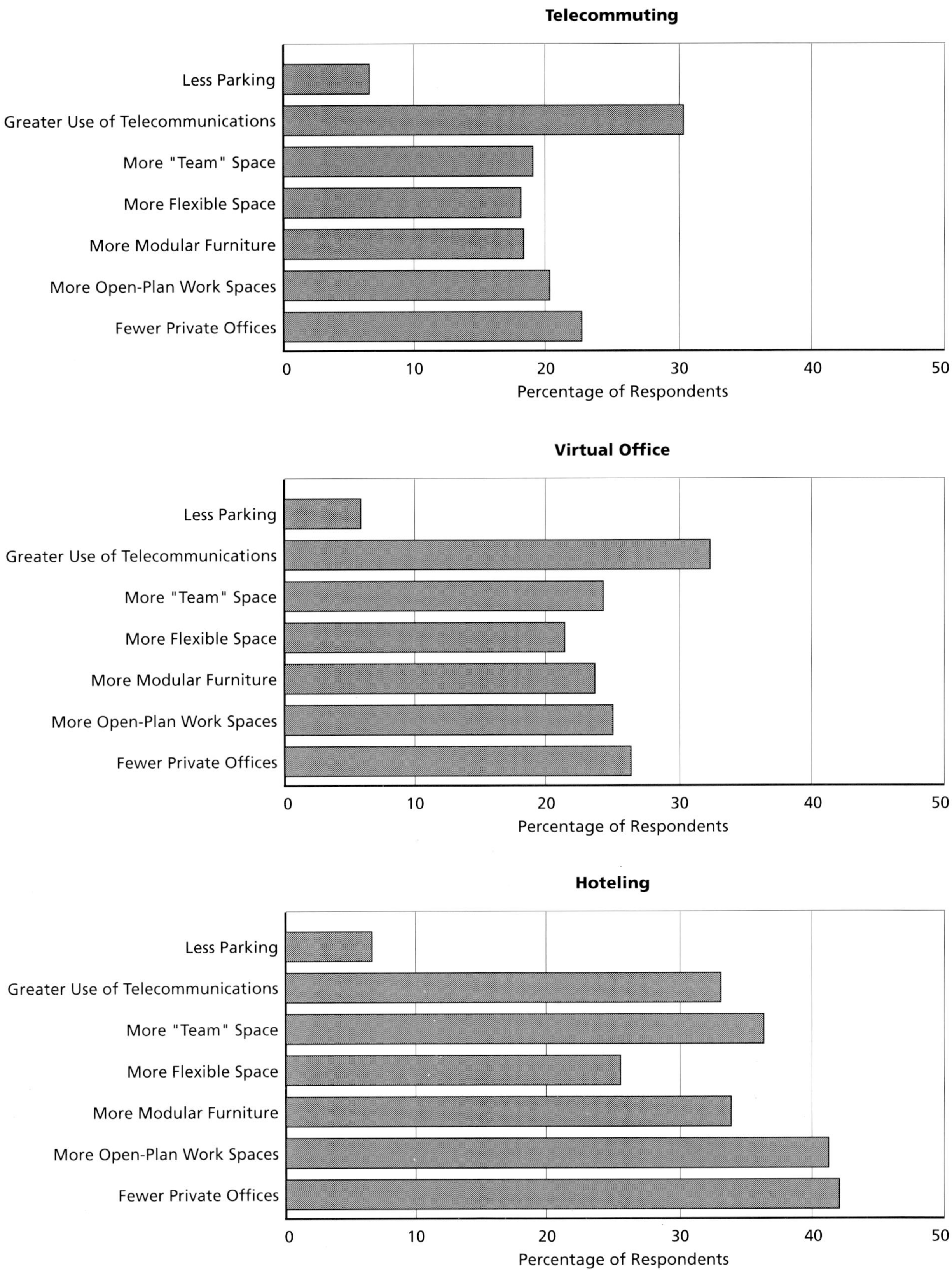

A higher percentage of high-tech firms, accountants, insurance firms, and consultants than other types of businesses use at least one alternative office strategy (Figure 5-4).

- High-tech firms are the top users of alternative office strategies. Almost one-half use telecommuting, 37 percent use virtual offices, and 7 percent use hoteling.

- Accountants are one of the top users of alternative office strategies. About 35 percent use telecommuting, 33 percent use virtual offices, and 21 percent use hoteling.

- Insurance firms are one of the top users of telecommuting (43 percent of respondents), moderate users of virtual offices (25 percent of respondents), and only minor users of hoteling (8 percent).

- Consultants have a relatively high rate of using alternative office strategies. About 33 percent use telecommuting, 31 percent use virtual offices, and 11 percent use hoteling.

- Engineers are moderately high users of alternative office strategies: 29 percent use telecommuting, 26 percent use virtual offices, and 8 percent use hoteling.

- Financial services are moderate users of alternative office strategies. About 30 percent of financial services use telecommuting, 22 percent use virtual offices, and only 5 percent use hoteling.

- Communications firms are relatively moderate users of alternative office strategies. About 25 percent use telecommuting, 24 percent use virtual offices, and only 5 percent use hoteling.

- Government agencies are moderate users of only one alternative strategy—telecommuting, used by about 21 percent of government agencies. Only 8 percent use virtual offices, 5 percent hoteling.

- Nonprofit organizations are moderate users of just one alternative—telecommuting, used by about 23 percent. Only 10 percent use virtual offices, only 1 percent hoteling.

Figure 5-4 **Use of Alternative Office Strategies, by Business Group**

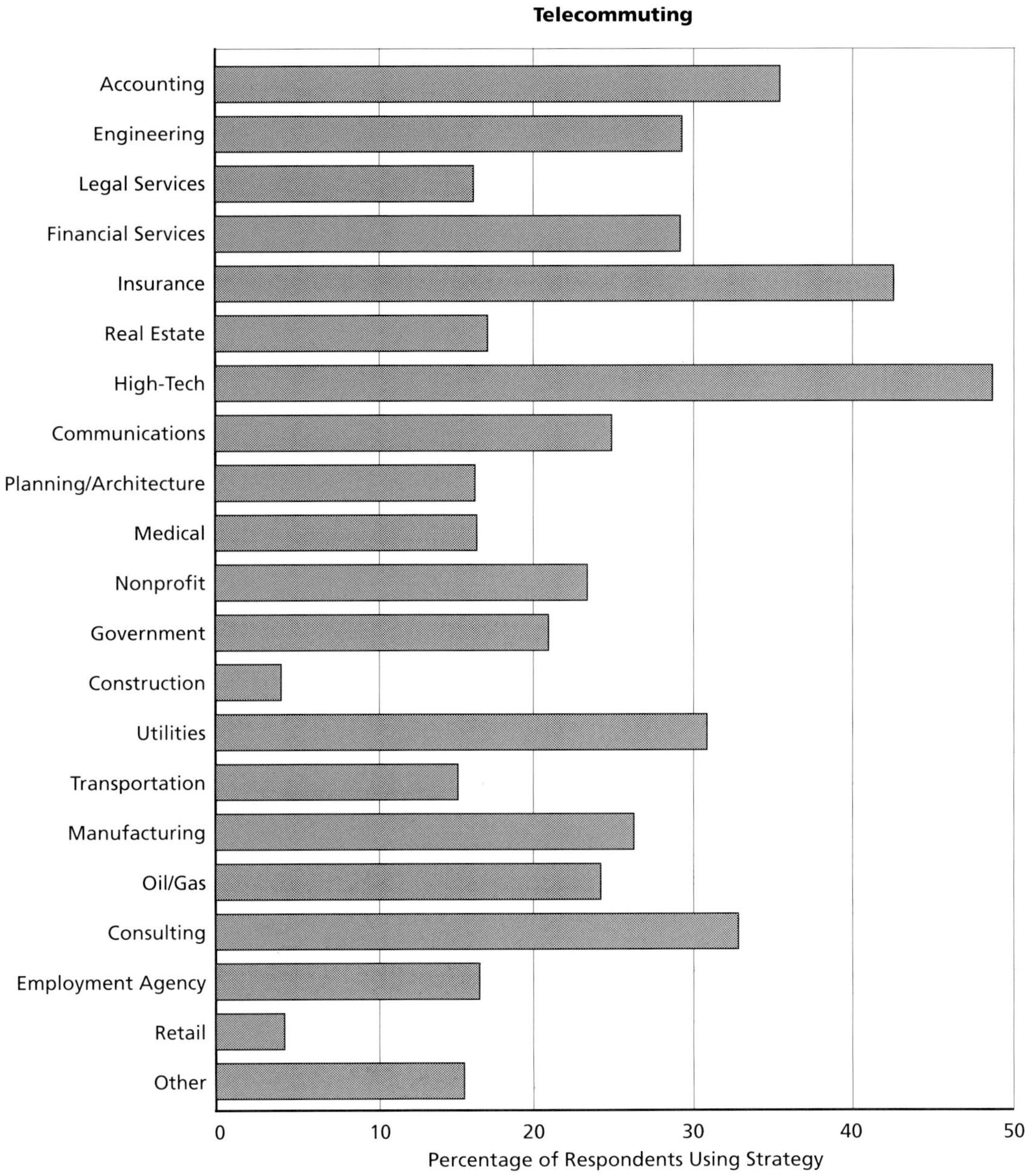

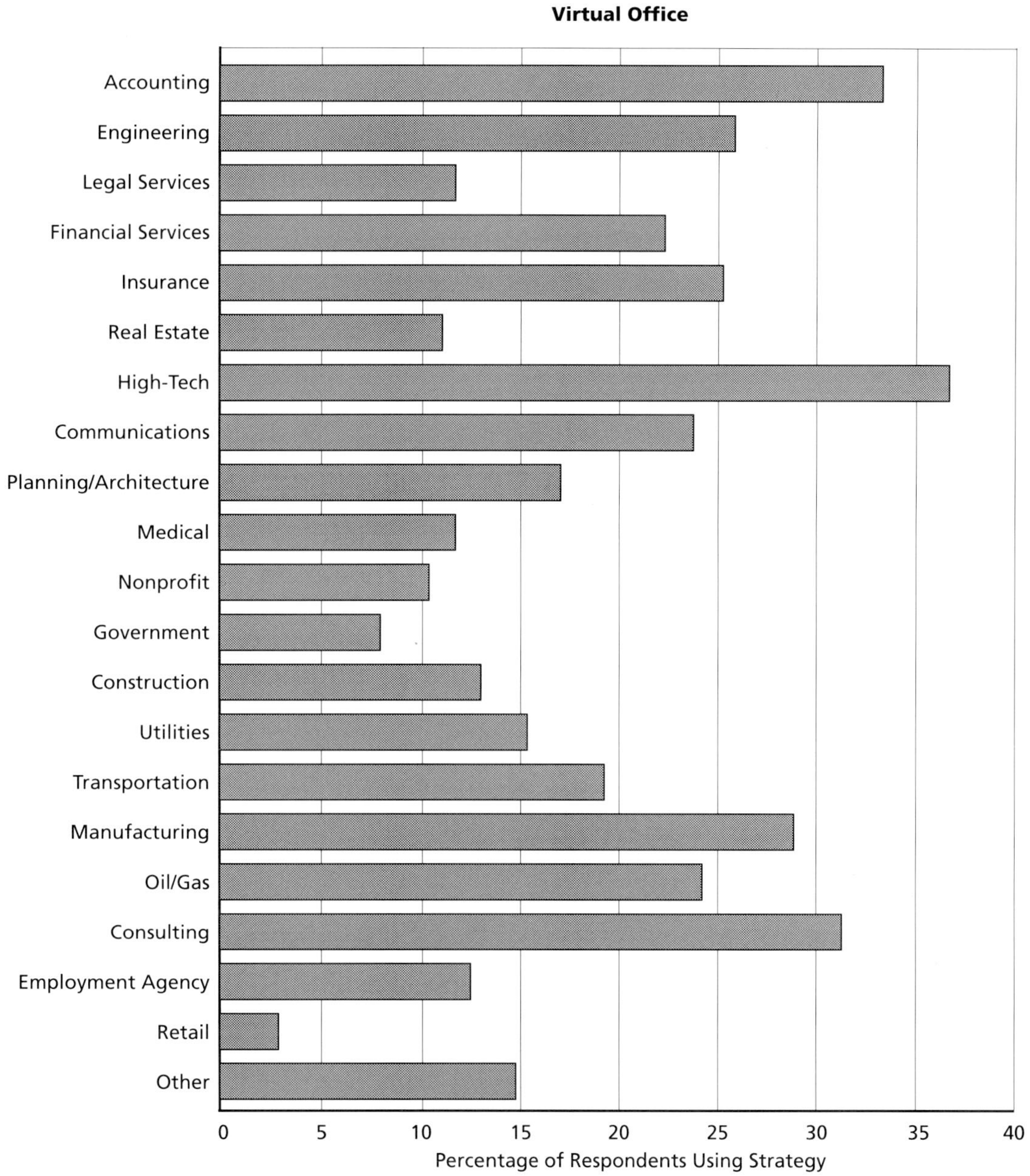
Virtual Office
Accounting
Engineering
Legal Services
Financial Services
Insurance
Real Estate
High-Tech
Communications
Planning/Architecture
Medical
Nonprofit
Government
Construction
Utilities
Transportation
Manufacturing
Oil/Gas
Consulting
Employment Agency
Retail
Other
0
5
10
15
20
25
30
35
40
Percentage of Respondents Using Strategy

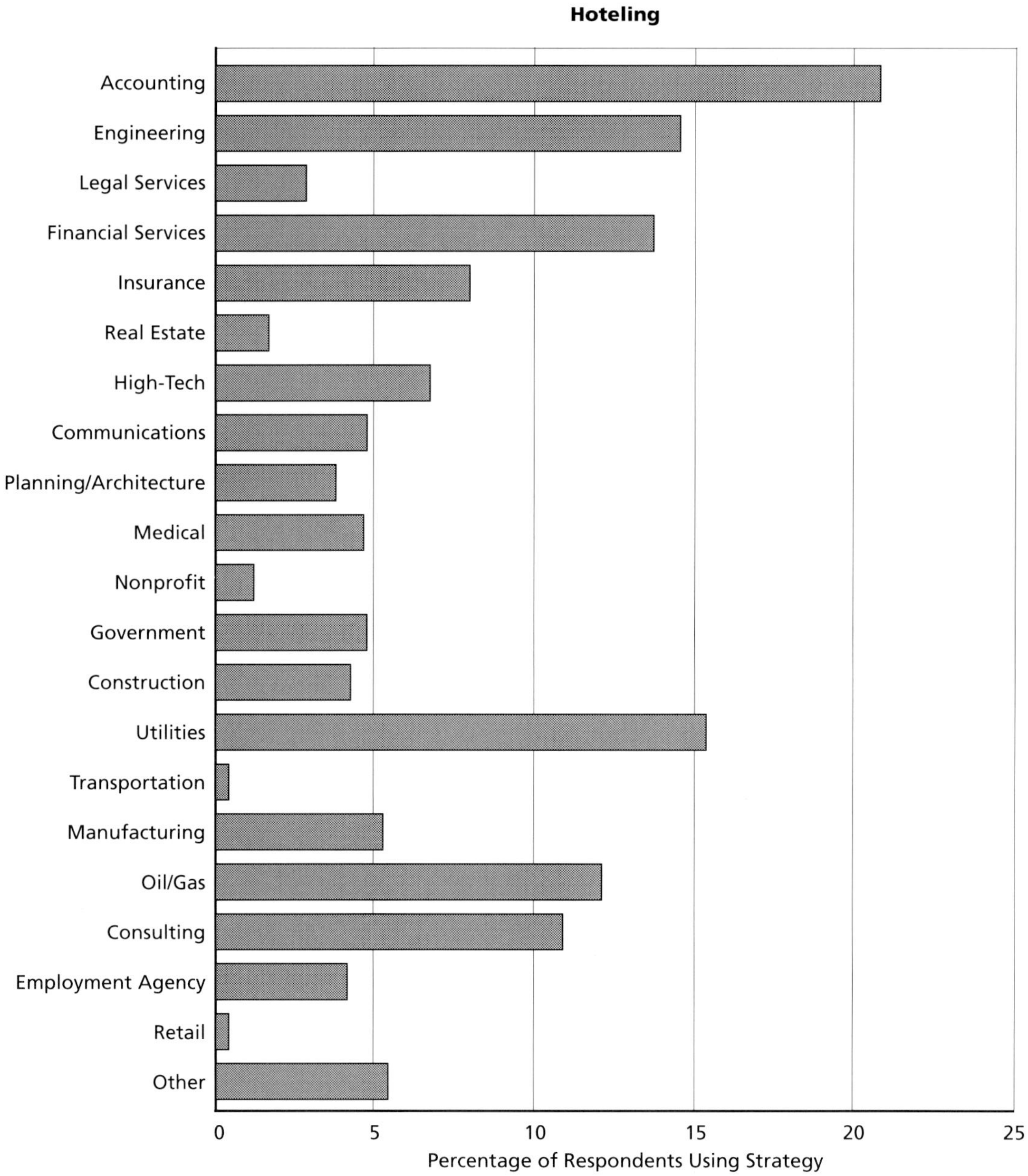
Hoteling
Accounting
Engineering
Legal Services
Financial Services
Insurance
Real Estate
High-Tech
Communications
Planning/Architecture
Medical
Nonprofit
Government
Construction
Utilities
Transportation
Manufacturing
Oil/Gas
Consulting
Employment Agency
Retail
Other
0
5
10
15
20
25
Percentage of Respondents Using Strategy

6

Highlights By Type Of Tenant

Using data discussed in the preceding chapters, this chapter provides a snapshot of each of the 14 largest business groups that responded to the survey (see also Appendix B). The remaining types of businesses are not discussed in detail, as responses were insufficient to draw statistically viable conclusions, but tabular information is included in Appendix B.

Each profile includes a summary with descriptive information about the size, expected changes in size, location, and tenure status (leasing versus owning), availability and importance of intelligent building features, the use of alternative office strategies, and the importance of and satisfaction with 51 building features, amenities, and services. The largest groups in descending order of total number of respondents are as follows:

- Financial services
- Legal services
- Real estate firms
- Planning/architecture firms
- High-tech firms
- Communications firms
- Insurance firms
- Medical services
- Nonprofit organizations
- Retail tenants
- Consulting firms
- Government agencies
- Engineering firms
- Accounting firms.

Financial Services

Most respondents in financial services are small, but the group exhibits a wide range of sizes. A majority (60 percent) have fewer than 20 employees, but close to 20 percent have more than 250 employees. This range is reflected in square footage: just over 60 percent of respondents are in spaces of 10,000 square feet or less, and slightly less than 20 percent are in spaces of more than 100,000 square feet.

One-half of respondents in financial services anticipate an increase in space required over the next three years, generally for no more than an additional 50 percent of the current space. Most others anticipate no change in space needed.

Just over one-half are in Class B buildings, and 43 percent are in Class A buildings. A small portion (15 percent) own their space.

Photo credit for page 61
The Durst Organization Headquarters
New York, New York
Reproduced with permission from *Corporate Interiors No. 1*
Design Firm: Environetics Group
Photography: Max Hilaire

About 64 percent are in downtowns, primarily in central cities. The balance of the financial service firms are located equally in office parks and other suburban locations.

The most important intelligent building features to financial service firms are wiring for high-speed networks, LAN/WAN connectivity, and high-tech, energy-efficient HVAC systems.

Financial services is among the business groups with the highest proportion of firms in buildings with certain intelligent features: LAN/WAN connectivity (36 percent of all financial service firms), conduits for power/data/voice cabling (33 percent), high-tech, energy-efficient HVAC systems (33 percent), redundant power source (22 percent), and satellite accessibility (20 percent).

Wiring for high-speed networks is important to 38 percent of financial service firms but is available in only 28 percent of their buildings. Therefore, by adding this feature to the building, building owners and managers can immediately affect these tenants' satisfaction with their office space.

Financial service firms are moderate users of alternative office strategies. About 30 percent of financial service firms use telecommuting, 22 percent use virtual offices, and only 5 percent use hoteling.

The importance of and satisfaction with 51 building features, amenities, and services for financial service firms are shown in Figure B-1 in Appendix B.

Legal Services

Most respondents providing legal services are quite small. Almost 70 percent have fewer than 20 employees; very few (8 percent) have more than 100 employees. This range is reflected in square footage of offices; just under 70 percent of respondents are located in spaces of 10,000 square feet or less.

Only 38 percent of respondents anticipate an increase in space required over the next three years, generally for no more than an additional 50 percent of the current space. Most other tenants anticipate no change in space needed.

Almost 62 percent of respondents are in Class B buildings, 33 percent in Class A buildings. Practically all the respondents providing legal services lease their office space.

The vast majority of legal service firms responding (82 percent) are in central city downtowns, with the balance located equally in all three suburban locations.

The most important intelligent building features for legal service firms are wiring for high-speed networks and high-tech, energy-efficient HVAC systems.

Despite the high ranking of some intelligent building features, relatively few legal service firms are located in buildings that provide them. Only 23 percent of their buildings have high-tech, energy-efficient HVAC systems, and only 17 percent have wiring for high-speed networks.

Relatively few legal service firms use alternative office strategies; in fact, legal service firms are among the lowest users of all business groups. Only 16 percent use telecommuting, 12 percent use virtual offices, and 3 percent use hoteling.

The importance of and satisfaction with 51 building features, amenities, and services for legal service firms are shown in Figure B-2 in Appendix B.

Real Estate Firms

Most respondents in real estate are quite small. About 70 percent have fewer than 20 employees; very few (10 percent) have more than 100 employees. This range is reflected in the square footage of office space: 75 percent of tenants are located in spaces of 10,000 square feet or less.

Almost one-half anticipate an increase in space required over the next three years, generally for no more than an additional 50 percent of the current space. Most of the other half anticipate no change in the amount of space needed.

About 55 percent are in Class B buildings, 36 percent in Class A buildings. A small portion (13 percent) own their space.

About 41 percent of responding real estate firms are located in central city downtowns; 27 percent are located in the suburbs other than in suburban downtowns and office parks. The balance is almost equally divided between suburban downtowns and office parks.

The most important intelligent building features for real estate firms are high-tech, energy-efficient HVAC systems, fiber-optics capability, conduits for power/data/voice cabling, and wiring for high-speed networks.

In general, respondents' current buildings do not completely follow their ranking of importance of intelligent features. Real estate firms are located in buildings with high-tech, energy-efficient HVAC systems (31 percent), conduits for power/data/voice cabling (24 percent), built-in wiring for Internet access (23 percent), fiber-optics capability (23 percent), LAN/WAN connectivity (22 percent), and wiring for high-speed networks (20 percent).

Relatively few responding real estate firms use alternative office strategies; in fact, real estate is among the lowest users of all business groups. Only 17 percent of responding real estate firms use telecommuting, 11 percent use virtual offices, and 2 percent use hoteling.

The importance of and satisfaction with 51 building features, amenities, and services for real estate firms are shown in Figure B-3 in Appendix B.

Planning/ Architecture Firms

Most responding planning/architecture firms are very small. Just over 70 percent of planning/architecture firms have fewer than 20 employees, and very few (12 percent) have more than 40. This range is reflected in the square footage of offices: 79 percent of responding planning/architecture firms are located in spaces of 10,000 square feet or less.

About 55 percent anticipate an increase in space required over the next three years, generally for no more than an additional 50 percent of the current space. Most other respondents anticipate no change in space needed.

Just under 59 percent of responding planning/architecture firms are located in Class B buildings, 22 percent are in Class A buildings, and 20 percent are in Class C buildings. This category has the highest proportion among all business groups of tenants in Class C buildings. A small portion (10 percent) own their office space.

Just under 60 percent are located in central city downtowns, with the balance almost equally divided among suburban downtowns, office parks, and other suburban locations.

A relatively moderate number of respondents in planning/architecture are located in buildings with built-in wiring for Internet access (24 percent), conduits for power/data/voice cabling (23 percent), wiring for high-speed networks (22 percent), and LAN/WAN connectivity (21 percent). Only 16 percent have ISDN and 15 percent high-tech, energy-efficient HVAC systems in their buildings.

Despite the relatively low number of firms with high-tech, energy-efficient HVAC systems in their buildings, 46 percent of respondents rank this feature in the top three most important to their organization. Similarly, 35 percent rank wiring for high-speed networks and 31 percent rank conduits for power/data/voice cabling among the three most important intelligent building features.

Relatively few planning/architecture firms use alternative office strategies. In fact, planning/architecture firms have among the lowest rates of use of all business groups. Only 16 percent use telecommuting, 8 percent use virtual offices, and 4 percent use hoteling.

The importance of and satisfaction with 51 building features, amenities, and services for planning/architecture firms are shown in Figure B-4 in Appendix B.

High-Tech Firms

The primary function of 44 percent of responding high-tech firms is research and development. They tend to be small firms, but the group exhibits a range of sizes. Just over 60 percent of high-tech firms have fewer than 20 employees; close to 20 percent have more than 100 employees. This range is reflected in square footage, with 62 percent of respondents in spaces of 10,000 square feet or less.

Almost 60 percent anticipate an increase in space required over the next three years, with 75 percent of them anticipating the need for no more than an additional 50 percent of the current space and 25 percent anticipating up to an additional 150 percent. Most other tenants anticipate no change in space needed.

Almost two-thirds of responding high-tech firms are located in Class B buildings, 25 percent in Class A buildings. Practically all responding high-tech firms lease their office space.

One-third are located in office parks, and about 22 percent are located in each of the other three locations—central city downtowns, suburban downtowns, and other suburban locations.

The most important intelligent building features for high-tech firms are wiring for high-speed networks, LAN/WAN connectivity, and built-in wiring for Internet access.

Generally, the choice of location for these firms is in line with the ranking of intelligent building features. High-tech firms is one of the business groups with the highest proportion of firms in buildings with LAN/WAN connectivity, wiring for high-speed networks, and built-in wiring for Internet access, ISDN, and a redundant power source. Moreover, 25 percent of high-tech firms are located in buildings with high-tech, energy-efficient HVAC systems, 20 percent in buildings with fiber-optics capability.

High-tech firms are the top users of alternative office strategies. Almost one-half use telecommuting, 37 percent use virtual offices, and 15 percent use hoteling.

The importance of and satisfaction with 51 building features, amenities, and services for high-tech firms are shown in Figure B-5 in Appendix B.

Communications Firms

The majority of responding communications firms are small, but the group exhibits a range of sizes. Almost 70 percent of communications firms have fewer than 20 employees, but close to 20 percent have more than 100 employees. This range is reflected in square footage, with 70 percent of tenants in spaces of 10,000 square feet or less.

Only 37 percent anticipate an increase in space required over the next three years, generally for no more than an additional 50 percent of current space. Most of the remainder anticipate no change in space needed.

About 55 percent of responding communications firms are located in Class B buildings, 37 percent in Class A buildings. Practically all communications firms lease their office space.

Over three-quarters are located in central city (62 percent) and suburban (15 percent) downtowns. The remainder are found in office parks and other suburban locations.

The most important intelligent building features to communications firms are a redundant power source, wiring for high-speed networks, built-in wiring for Internet access, and fiber-optics capability.

Except for redundant power sources, the current availability of intelligent building features reflects the relative importance of the features: 28 percent of responding communications firms are located in buildings with built-in wiring for Internet access, 26 percent in buildings with fiber-optics capability, 24 percent in buildings with conduits for power/data/voice cabling, and 23 percent in buildings with ISDN.

Communications firms are relatively moderate users of alternative office strategies. About 25 percent use telecommuting, 24 percent use virtual offices, and only 5 percent use hoteling.

The importance of and satisfaction with 51 building features, amenities, and services for communications firms are shown in Figure B-6 in Appendix B.

Insurance Firms

Sizes of responding insurance firms vary widely. Just over 50 percent have fewer than 20 employees, 33 percent more than 100. This range is reflected in square footage of offices, with 54 percent of respondents in spaces of 10,000 square feet or less and 21 percent in spaces of more than 60,000 square feet.

Only 33 percent of responding insurance firms anticipate an increase in space required over the next three years, generally for no more than an additional 50 percent of the current space. Most other tenants anticipate no change in space needed.

One-half of respondents are located in Class B buildings, 42 percent in Class A buildings. A small portion (8 percent) owns their space office.

Just over one-half are located in central city downtowns; the balance is almost equally divided among all three suburban locations.

Insurance firms are among the highest users of intelligent building features: 40 percent of respondents have built-in wiring for Internet access and LAN/WAN connectivity; 35 percent have fiber-optics capability and wiring for high-speed networks; 26 percent have high-tech, energy-efficient HVAC systems and automatic on/off sensors for lights; and 21 percent have ISDN, a redundant power source, and satellite accessibility.

Thirty-seven percent rank high-tech, energy-efficient HVAC systems among the top three features, but only 26 percent are located in buildings with that feature—a finding to remember when marketing a building to insurance firms. The importance and availability of most other features coincide with rankings.

Insurance firms are among the top users of telecommuting, with 43 percent of respondents using this alternative office strategy. They are moderate users of virtual offices (25 percent of respondents), and only a minor user of hoteling (8 percent).

The importance of and satisfaction with 51 building features, amenities, and services for insurance firms are shown in Figure B-7 in Appendix B.

Medical Services

The vast majority of respondents offering medical services are small; about 85 percent of tenants in medical services have fewer than 20 employees, and 71 percent have fewer than ten. None of the respondents have more than 500 employees. This range is reflected in square footage of office space; 83 percent of respondents are located in spaces of 10,000 square feet or less.

Only 29 percent of respondents offering medical services anticipate an increase in space required over the next three years, generally for no more than an additional 50 percent of the current space. Most other respondents anticipate no change in space needed.

Almost 60 percent are located in Class B buildings, 32 percent in Class A buildings. Almost all medical services own their space.

Medical services are fairly evenly distributed across central city downtowns, suburban downtowns, office parks, and other suburban locations.

Very few medical services (no more than 13 percent) are located in buildings with any of the intelligent features listed in the survey.

Relatively few medical firms use alternative office strategies; in fact, medical services as a category has among the lowest rates of use of all business groups. Only 16 percent use telecommuting, 12 percent use virtual offices, and 5 percent use hoteling.

The importance of and satisfaction with 51 building features, amenities, and services for medical services are shown in Figure B-8 in Appendix B.

Nonprofit Organizations

The majority of responding nonprofits are small. Just over 70 percent have fewer than 20 employees, and very few (12 percent) have more than 40 employees. This range is reflected in square footage; 77 percent of respondents are located in spaces of 10,000 square feet or less.

About 43 percent of responding nonprofits anticipate an increase in space required over the next three years, generally for no more than an additional 50 percent of current space. Most other respondents anticipate no change in the amount of space needed.

About 60 percent of responding nonprofits are located in Class B buildings, 34 percent in Class A buildings. Practically all nonprofits lease their office space.

Almost 90 percent of nonprofits are located in downtowns, both central city (70 percent) and suburban (18 percent).

The two most important intelligent building features for nonprofits are built-in wiring for Internet access and wiring for high-speed networks. The relative importance of these two features is not reflected in their current availability. A relatively moderate number of nonprofits are located in buildings with high-tech, energy-efficient HVAC systems, Internet access, and wiring for high-speed networks.

Nonprofits are moderate users of telecommuting—about 23 percent of responding firms—but only 10 percent use virtual offices and only 1 percent use hoteling.

The importance of and satisfaction with 51 building features, amenities, and services for nonprofit organizations are shown in Figure B-9 in Appendix B.

Retail Tenants

The vast majority of responding retail tenants are small. About 82 percent of retailers have fewer than 20 employees; very few (11 percent) have more than 40 employees. This range is reflected in square footage of office space, with 85 percent of respondents in spaces of 10,000 square feet or less.

Only 33 percent anticipate an increase in space required over the next three years, generally for no more than an additional 50 percent of current space. Most other tenants anticipate no change in space needed.

Just over 60 percent of responding retailers are located in Class B buildings, 32 percent in Class A buildings. Practically all retailers lease their space.

Almost one-half of responding retailers are located in central city downtowns, the rest divided fairly evenly among all suburban locations.

Very few retailers are located in buildings with intelligent building features. No more than 12 percent of retailers have any of the features listed in the survey.

As might be expected, very few (less than 4 percent) of responding retailers use telecommuting or virtual offices. No retailers use hoteling.

The importance of and satisfaction with 51 building features, amenities, and services for retailers are shown in Figure B-10 in Appendix B.

Consulting Firms

The majority of responding consulting firms are small. Just over 70 percent of respondents have fewer than 20 employees, and very few (12 percent) have more than 100 employees. This range is reflected in square footage of office space, with 73 percent of respondents in spaces of 10,000 square feet or less.

About 46 percent anticipate an increase in space required over the next three years, none of them for more than an additional 50 percent of current space. Most other tenants anticipate no change in space needed.

Almost two-thirds of respondents are located in Class B buildings, 26 percent in Class A buildings. All consulting companies lease their office space.

About two-thirds are found in downtown locations, primarily the central city. The remainder are equally divided between office parks and other suburban locations (not downtown).

The most important intelligent building features for consulting firms are built-in wiring for Internet access, ISDN, and wiring for high-speed networks. The importance of these features is not reflected in the current availability of intelligent buildings; relatively few consulting firms are located in buildings with these features.

Consultants are relatively high users of alternative office strategies: about 33 percent use telecommuting, 31 percent use virtual offices, and 11 percent use hoteling.

The importance of and satisfaction with 51 building features, amenities, and services for consulting firms are shown in Figure B-11 in Appendix B.

Government Agencies

Sizes of government agencies vary widely. Just under 40 percent of responding government agencies have fewer than 20 employees, about 20 percent have 20 to 100 employees, about 20 percent have 100 to 500 employees, and about 20 percent have more than 500 employees. This range is reflected in square footage of office space: 38 percent of respondents are located in spaces of 10,000 square feet or less, 26 percent in spaces from 10,000 to 60,000 square feet, and 36 percent in spaces over 60,000 square feet.

Only 36 percent of respondents anticipate an increase in space required over the next three years, generally for no more than an additional 30 percent of current space. Not surprisingly, given the move to downsize and/or consolidate government operations, 21 percent of tenants anticipate a decrease in space required.

Just over 70 percent of respondents are located in Class B buildings, 27 percent in Class A buildings. A small portion (5 percent) own their space.

The vast majority (81 percent) are located in central city and suburban downtowns. The remainder are found in office parks and other suburban locations outside downtown.

The top-ranked intelligent building features for responding government agencies are LAN/WAN connectivity, wiring for high-speed networks, and fiber-optics capability.

Government agencies, reflecting this ranking, are among the business groups with the highest proportion of respondents in buildings with LAN/WAN connectivity (44 percent of all respondents), wiring for high-speed networks (40 percent), and fiber-optics capability (32 percent).

Government agencies are moderate users of only one alternative office strategy; about 21 percent of responding government agencies use telecommuting. Only 8 percent use virtual offices, and 5 percent use hoteling.

The importance of and satisfaction with 51 building features, amenities, and services for government agencies are shown in Figure B-12 in Appendix B.

Engineering Firms

The primary function of over one-third of responding engineering firms is research and development. Size of respondents varies widely; just under 50 percent have fewer than 20 employees, 24 percent have 20 to 100 employees, and the rest have more than 100 employees. This range is reflected in square footage of office space, with 52 percent of respondents in spaces of 10,000 square feet or less, 35 percent in spaces of 10,000 to 60,000 square feet, and the rest in spaces over 60,000 square feet.

About one-half (55 percent) anticipate an increase in space required over the next three years, with 86 percent anticipating the need for no more than an additional 50 percent of current space and 14 percent anticipating the need for up to 100 percent more space. Most other tenants anticipate no change in space needed.

About 70 percent of responding engineering firms are located in Class B buildings, 22 percent in Class A buildings. A small portion (5 percent) own their office space.

A strong minority (41 percent) are located in central city downtowns, 28 percent in office parks. The other firms are equally divided between suburban downtowns and other suburban locations outside office parks.

A relatively moderate number of responding engineering firms are located in buildings with LAN/WAN connectivity (24 percent), built-in wiring for Internet access (22 percent), conduits for power/data/voice cabling (21 percent), and wiring for high-speed networks (21 percent). Only 17 percent are located in buildings with fiber-optics capability and high-tech, energy-efficient HVAC systems, 16 percent in buildings with a redundant power source and automatic sensors in faucets and toilets.

A moderately high percentage of engineering firms use alternative office strategies: 29 percent use telecommuting, 26 percent use virtual offices, and 8 percent use hoteling.

The importance of and satisfaction with 51 building features, amenities, and services for engineering firms are shown in Figure B-13 in Appendix B.

Accounting Firms

The majority of responding accounting firms are small; just over 70 percent of accounting firms have fewer than 20 employees, and very few (13 percent) have more than 100 employees. This range is reflected in square footage of office space, with 74 percent of respondents in spaces of 10,000 square feet or less.

Only 34 percent of responding accounting firms anticipate an increase in space required over the next three years; 86 percent of them anticipate the need for no more than an additional 50 percent of current space, and 14 percent anticipate needing up to an additional 150 percent. Most other tenants anticipate no change in space needed.

Almost 60 percent are located in Class B buildings, 30 percent in Class A buildings. All accounting firms lease their office space.

Almost 60 percent of responding accounting firms are located in downtowns, and almost exclusively central city downtowns. Other firms are divided equally between office parks and other suburban locations outside downtowns.

Relatively few accountants are located in buildings with intelligent features, with the exception of the 21 percent that are located in buildings with high-tech, energy-efficient HVAC systems. Only 17 percent are located in buildings with wiring for high-speed networks, 15 percent in buildings with built-in wiring for Internet access, LAN/WAN connectivity, and conduits for power/data/voice cabling.

Accountants are one of the top users of alternative office strategies. About 43 percent use telecommuting, 33 percent use virtual offices, and 21 percent use hoteling.

The importance of and satisfaction with 51 building features, amenities, and services for accounting firms are shown in Figure B-14 in Appendix B. Similar information for the remaining types of businesses (construction, utilities, transportation, manufacturing, oil/gas companies, employment agencies, and "other") is shown in Figures B-15 through B-21, respectively.

Appendix A

Survey Questionnaire

BOMA/ULI Office Tenant Survey

BOMA INTERNATIONAL

ULI

I. General Information

1. **How long has your organization been in your current office space?** (Check one.)

☐ Less than one year
☐ 1 to 3 years
☐ 4 to 5 years
☐ 6 to 10 years
☐ More than 10 years

2. **Does your organization lease or own your current office space?** (Check one.)

☐ Lease
☐ Own

3. **In what city and state/province is your office space located?**

City ______________________ State/Province______________________

4. **Location of your building.** (Check one.)

☐ Central city downtown
☐ Surburban downtown
☐ Office park
☐ Other suburban location

5. **What type of business does your organization operate?** (Check *one* only.)

☐ Accounting
☐ Engineering
☐ Legal services
☐ Financial services
☐ Insurance
☐ Real estate
☐ High-technology
☐ Communications
☐ Planning/architecture
☐ Medical
☐ Nonprofit
☐ Government
☐ Construction
☐ Utilities
☐ Transportation
☐ Manufacturing
☐ Other (specify): ______________________

6. **Would you categorize the *primary* function of your business operations at this location as any of the following?** (Check yes or no.)

	Yes	No
Data processing/customer service	☐	☐
Telemarketing	☐	☐
Research and development	☐	☐

Photo credit for page 75
Law Offices of Wachtell, Lipton, Rosen & Katz
New York, New York
Reproduced with permission from *Corporate Interiors No. 1*
Design Firm: Gensler
Photography: Marco Lorenzetti, Hedrich Blessing

II. Office Building Features and Amenities

How important are the following building features and amenities to your organization? Please circle a number on the scale of 1 to 5 to indicate the relative *importance* of each feature.

How satisfied are you in your current building with these building features and amenities? Please circle a number on the scale of 1 to 5 to indicate your relative *satisfaction* with each feature. Leave blank if the feature is not applicable to your building or organization.

	IMPORTANCE TO YOUR ORGANIZATION					YOUR LEVEL OF SATISFACTION				
	Not Important	←		→	Very Important	Not Satisfied	←		→	Very Satisfied
Locational Features										
Suburban location	1	2	3	4	5	1	2	3	4	5
Downtown location	1	2	3	4	5	1	2	3	4	5
Proximity to clients	1	2	3	4	5	1	2	3	4	5
Proximity to business services	1	2	3	4	5	1	2	3	4	5
Proximity to where employees live	1	2	3	4	5	1	2	3	4	5
Proximity to restaurants/retail/personal services	1	2	3	4	5	1	2	3	4	5
Proximity to public transportation	1	2	3	4	5	1	2	3	4	5
General Building Features										
Rental rates (including pass-throughs/escalations)	1	2	3	4	5	1	2	3	4	5
Operating expenses	1	2	3	4	5	1	2	3	4	5
Tenant improvement allowance	1	2	3	4	5	1	2	3	4	5
Tenant mix	1	2	3	4	5	1	2	3	4	5
On-site parking	1	2	3	4	5	1	2	3	4	5
Covered parking	1	2	3	4	5	1	2	3	4	5
Cost of parking	1	2	3	4	5	1	2	3	4	5
Disabled access	1	2	3	4	5	1	2	3	4	5
Environmentally friendly building systems and materials	1	2	3	4	5	1	2	3	4	5
Image and prestige of the building	1	2	3	4	5	1	2	3	4	5
Features of Building Exterior										
Appearance of building	1	2	3	4	5	1	2	3	4	5
Appearance of grounds/landscaping	1	2	3	4	5	1	2	3	4	5
Outside signage for your organization	1	2	3	4	5	1	2	3	4	5
Outside loading docks	1	2	3	4	5	1	2	3	4	5
Roof-loading capability	1	2	3	4	5	1	2	3	4	5
Operable windows	1	2	3	4	5	1	2	3	4	5
Features of Interior Common Areas										
Building-wide security systems during work day	1	2	3	4	5	1	2	3	4	5
Building-wide security systems after hours	1	2	3	4	5	1	2	3	4	5
Appearance of entry lobby (style/finishes)	1	2	3	4	5	1	2	3	4	5
Appearance of common areas other than lobby	1	2	3	4	5	1	2	3	4	5
Elevator service speed	1	2	3	4	5	1	2	3	4	5

	Importance to Your Organization					Your Level of Satisfaction				
	Not Important	←		→	**Very Important**	**Not Satisfied**	←		→	**Very Satisfied**
Features of Your Office Suite										
Indoor air quality	1	2	3	4	5	1	2	3	4	5
Acoustics/noise control	1	2	3	4	5	1	2	3	4	5
Power capacity	1	2	3	4	5	1	2	3	4	5
Comfortable temperature	1	2	3	4	5	1	2	3	4	5
Tenant control of temperature	1	2	3	4	5	1	2	3	4	5
Cost of after-hours heating/cooling	1	2	3	4	5	1	2	3	4	5
Proximity to elevators	1	2	3	4	5	1	2	3	4	5
Proximity to restrooms	1	2	3	4	5	1	2	3	4	5
Security/controlled access	1	2	3	4	5	1	2	3	4	5
Flexible suite layout (e.g., easily reconfigured)	1	2	3	4	5	1	2	3	4	5
Building Amenities										
Banking/ATM	1	2	3	4	5	1	2	3	4	5
Child-care facility	1	2	3	4	5	1	2	3	4	5
Concierge	1	2	3	4	5	1	2	3	4	5
Fitness center	1	2	3	4	5	1	2	3	4	5
Food service	1	2	3	4	5	1	2	3	4	5
Convenience retail stores	1	2	3	4	5	1	2	3	4	5
Shared business services (e.g., data and word processing)	1	2	3	4	5	1	2	3	4	5
Shared videoconference facility	1	2	3	4	5	1	2	3	4	5
Shared teleconference facility	1	2	3	4	5	1	2	3	4	5
Other amenities (specify):										
______________________	1	2	3	4	5	1	2	3	4	5
______________________	1	2	3	4	5	1	2	3	4	5
Building Management										
On-site staff	1	2	3	4	5	1	2	3	4	5
Staff responsiveness	1	2	3	4	5	1	2	3	4	5
Staff ability to meet your needs	1	2	3	4	5	1	2	3	4	5
Effectiveness of management communications	1	2	3	4	5	1	2	3	4	5
Quality of maintenance work	1	2	3	4	5	1	2	3	4	5
On-site security guard	1	2	3	4	5	1	2	3	4	5

III. Intelligent Building Features

An intelligent building is one that provides a productive, cost-effective, comfortable environment for its tenants through the use of technologically advanced building systems and structural features.

1. **Does your building have any of the following intelligent building features?** Check all that apply in the Existing Feature column. Rank the three features that are most important to your organization (with #1 being the most important) in the Most Important Feature column.

	Existing Feature	Most Important Feature
Fiber-optics capability	☐	______
Built-in wiring for Internet access	☐	______
Wiring for high-speed networks	☐	______
LAN and WAN connectivity	☐	______
Satellite accessibility	☐	______
ISDN	☐	______
Redundant power source	☐	______
Conduits for power/data/voice cabling	☐	______
High-tech, energy-efficient HVAC system	☐	______
Automatic on/off sensor in the lighting system	☐	______
"Smart" elevators that group passengers by floor designation	☐	______
Automatic sensors installed in faucets/toilets	☐	______
Computerized/interactive building directory	☐	______

Other (specify): ______________________________

2. **Please specify any intelligent/high-technology building features that your organization needs but that are not available in your current building.** (If none, skip to Section IV.)

   a.______________________________

   b.______________________________

   c.______________________________

3. **If you responded to Question 2 above, would you be willing to pay additional rent to have the features mentioned made available?**

   ☐ No ☐ Yes (If yes, approximately how much additional rent? $ ______ per square foot)

IV. Alternative Office Strategies

1. **Many companies have adopted nontraditional work styles, often called alternative office strategies. Which, if any, of the following alternative office strategies does your company use?** (Check all that apply.)

☐ Hoteling (A practice in which some employees do not have a permanent desk. Employees are able to reserve space in the regular office facility by calling ahead, similar to booking a hotel room.)

☐ Telecommuting (A practice that allows employees to work at home on a regular basis during normal business hours. Such employees may also have permanent workspace in the company's office facility.)

☐ Virtual Office (The use of a personal computer with modem and fax capability, printer, and cellular telephone to allow employees to conduct work in nontraditional settings such as clients' offices. Such employees may also have permanent workspace in the company's office facility.)

☐ Other alternative office strategy (specify): ______________________________

☐ None (Skip to Section V below.)

2. **Approximately what percentage of employees at your office location participate in these programs?** _______% of the workforce.

3. **Rank the top three reasons (with #1 being the primary reason) that your organization implemented alternative office strategies.**

   _____ Employee demand

   _____ To reduce overhead costs

   _____ To increase operating efficiency

   _____ To reduce office space needs

   _____ Other (specify): ______________________________

4. **How have alternative office strategies affected the *amount* of office space your organization needs and the *configuration* of your office space?** (Check all that apply.)

Amount of Office Space (Square Footage)

- ☐ No change in amount of office space
- ☐ Realized up to a 10% net reduction in office space
- ☐ Realized more than a 10% net reduction in office space
- ☐ Realized an increase in office space

Configuration/Use of Office Space

- ☐ Have fewer private offices
- ☐ Have more open-plan work spaces
- ☐ Use more modular furniture systems
- ☐ Need more flexible office space
- ☐ Need more shared areas for project teams (e.g., small conference rooms)
- ☐ Make greater use of telecommunications technologies
- ☐ Need less parking

V. Your Current Office-Space Profile

1. **Approximately how many employees currently work for your organization at this location?** __________ employees.
2. **Approximately how many square feet of office space does your firm currently occupy in this building?** __________ square feet.
3. **How is your office space allocated?**
   ____% enclosed private offices ____% open-plan office space
4. **Do you currently sublease any of your office space to another tenant?** ☐ Yes ☐ No
5. **Do you anticipate any change in space needs in the next three years?**
   ☐ No change ☐ Increase by ______ % ☐ Decrease by ______ %
6. **If you were to renegotiate your lease today, how would you change the terms?** (Check all that apply.)
   ☐ Prefer shorter lease term ☐ Prefer longer lease term ☐ Negotiate a sublease clause ☐ Include a provision for expansion
7. **How would you rate your office building?** (Check the one that best fits.)
   ☐ Prime building (offers luxury amenities, high-quality standard finishes, state-of-the-art systems, exceptional accessibility, and definite market presence)
   ☐ Average building (offers basic amenities, fair- to good-quality finishes, and standard systems)
   ☐ Below-average building (dated, with few amenities; emphasis is on function)
8. **Is your organization inclined to stay in your building after your current lease expires?**
   ☐ Yes ☐ No ☐ Don't know
9. **Which category best represents your job function?**
   ☐ Principal/owner ☐ Department manager ☐ Administrative
   ☐ Executive ☐ Office manager ☐ Other (define): ____________________

Thank you for completing this survey!

Please return the questionnaire in the enclosed self-addressed envelope or send to the following address by **June 24, 1998:**

BOMA International
1201 New York Avenue, N.W.
Suite 300
Washington, D.C. 20005
Attn: Research Department

Appendix B

Preferences For Features, Amenities, And Services By Type of Business

Figure B-1

Importance of and Satisfaction with Building Features, Amenities, and Services for Financial Service Firms

	Important (Percent)	Satisfied (Percent)
Locational Features		
Proximity to business services	86	97
Proximity to where employees live	82	93
Proximity to restaurants/retail/personal services	80	90
Proximity to clients	74	96
Proximity to public transportation	75	92
General Building Features		
Rental rates (including pass-throughs/escalations)	97	90
Operating expenses	99	89
Image and prestige of the building	95	91
On-site parking	94	80
Tenant improvement allowance	94	83
Cost of parking	91	70
Environmentally friendly building systems and materials	93	88
Disabled access	83	95
Covered parking	84	76
Tenant mix	74	90
Features of Building Exterior		
Appearance of building	100	94
Appearance of grounds/landscaping	99	96
Outside signage for your organization	83	84
Outside loading docks	61	85
Operable windows	39	66
Roof-loading capacity	35	84
Features of Interior Common Areas		
Appearance of entry lobby (style/finishes)	98	90
Buildingwide security systems after hours	100	88
Appearance of common areas other than lobby	98	83
Elevator service speed	93	79
Buildingwide security systems during work day	97	88
Features of Tenants' Office Suites		
Comfortable temperature	100	80
Indoor air quality	100	86
Acoustics/noise control	99	85
Power capacity	98	95
Tenant control of temperature	95	69
Security/controlled access	98	91
Proximity to restrooms	94	94
Flexible suite layout (e.g., easily reconfigured)	96	87
Cost of after-hours heating/cooling	93	85
Proximity to elevators	89	96
Building Amenities		
Food service	84	72
Banking/ATM	82	81
Convenience retail stores	66	88
Fitness center	57	60
Child-care facility	53	56
Concierge	48	77
Shared videoconference facility	40	73
Shared teleconference facility	37	73
Shared business services (e.g., data and word processing)	37	80
Building Management		
Quality of building maintenance work	100	93
Building management's ability to meet your needs	92	93
Building management's responsiveness	100	92
Effectiveness of communications with building management	99	93
On-site building management staff	96	94
On-site security guard	97	89

Note: The numbers in the first column represent the percentage of respondents to whom a particular feature is important, the numbers in the second column the percentage of respondents who are satisfied with the feature as currently available.

Photo credit for page 81

Comerica, Inc., Operations Center
Auburn Hills, Michigan

Reproduced with permission from *Corporate Interiors No. 1*

Design Firm: Harley Ellington Design

Photography: Gary Quesada, Korab Hedrich Blessing

Figure B-2

Importance of and Satisfaction with Building Features, Amenities, and Services for Legal Service Firms

	Important (Percent)	Satisfied (Percent)
Locational Features		
Proximity to business services	92	98
Proximity to where employees live	73	97
Proximity to restaurants/retail/personal services	81	91
Proximity to clients	83	98
Proximity to public transportation	76	94
General Building Features		
Rental rates (including pass-throughs/escalations)	100	89
Operating expenses	99	89
Image and prestige of the building	95	92
On-site parking	93	81
Tenant improvement allowance	96	87
Cost of parking	93	74
Environmentally friendly building systems and materials	88	90
Disabled access	81	91
Covered parking	88	85
Tenant mix	79	95
Features of Building Exterior		
Appearance of building	99	94
Appearance of grounds/landscaping	98	90
Outside signage for your organization	64	79
Outside loading docks	59	86
Operable windows	36	67
Roof-loading capacity	17	82
Features of Interior Common Areas		
Appearance of entry lobby (style/finishes)	99	90
Buildingwide security systems after hours	98	86
Appearance of common areas other than lobby	98	84
Elevator service speed	99	71
Buildingwide security systems during work day	93	87
Features of Tenants' Office Suites		
Comfortable temperature	100	67
Indoor air quality	96	78
Acoustics/noise control	99	79
Power capacity	97	94
Tenant control of temperature	96	60
Security/controlled access	94	95
Proximity to restrooms	96	97
Flexible suite layout (e.g., easily reconfigured)	85	92
Cost of after-hours heating/cooling	89	76
Proximity to elevators	92	100
Building Amenities		
Food service	79	67
Banking/ATM	79	81
Convenience retail stores	69	75
Fitness center	60	71
Child-care facility	44	60
Concierge	52	86
Shared videoconference facility	36	65
Shared teleconference facility	32	68
Shared business services (e.g., data and word processing)	24	78
Building Management		
Quality of building maintenance work	94	94
Building management's ability to meet your needs	99	92
Building management's responsiveness	99	92
Effectiveness of communications with building management	99	85
On-site building management staff	98	93
On-site security guard	96	89

Note: The numbers in the first column represent the percentage of respondents to whom a particular feature is important, the numbers in the second column the percentage of respondents who are satisfied with the feature as currently available.

Figure B-3

Importance of and Satisfaction with Building Features, Amenities, and Services for Real Estate Firms

	Important (Percent)	Satisfied (Percent)
Locational Features		
Proximity to business services	92	100
Proximity to where employees live	87	94
Proximity to restaurants/retail/personal services	90	96
Proximity to clients	74	98
Proximity to public transportation	51	90
General Building Features		
Rental rates (including pass-throughs/escalations)	98	91
Operating expenses	98	88
Image and prestige of the building	95	92
On-site parking	92	84
Tenant improvement allowance	92	87
Cost of parking	91	85
Environmentally friendly building systems and materials	77	89
Disabled access	58	95
Covered parking	72	76
Tenant mix	65	95
Features of Building Exterior		
Appearance of building	96	91
Appearance of grounds/landscaping	98	91
Outside signage for your organization	56	85
Outside loading docks	29	87
Operable windows	32	75
Roof-loading capacity	13	89
Features of Interior Common Areas		
Appearance of entry lobby (style/finishes)	95	87
Buildingwide security systems after hours	93	86
Appearance of common areas other than lobby	95	82
Elevator service speed	82	72
Buildingwide security systems during work day	71	90
Features of Tenants' Office Suites		
Comfortable temperature	99	74
Indoor air quality	98	82
Acoustics/noise control	99	87
Power capacity	93	93
Tenant control of temperature	95	66
Security/controlled access	87	92
Proximity to restrooms	87	97
Flexible suite layout (e.g., easily reconfigured)	93	86
Cost of after-hours heating/cooling	82	85
Proximity to elevators	73	96
Building Amenities		
Food service	66	73
Banking/ATM	61	80
Convenience retail stores	69	83
Fitness center	50	59
Child-care facility	40	60
Concierge	40	70
Shared videoconference facility	31	65
Shared teleconference facility	29	67
Shared business services (e.g., data and word processing)	28	77
Building Management		
Quality of building maintenance work	98	85
Building management's ability to meet your needs	98	89
Building management's responsiveness	98	88
Effectiveness of communications with building management	98	86
On-site building management staff	85	84
On-site security guard	78	84

Note: The numbers in the first column represent the percentage of respondents to whom a particular feature is important, the numbers in the second column the percentage of respondents who are satisfied with the feature as currently available.

Figure B-4

Importance of and Satisfaction with Building Features, Amenities, and Services for Planning/Architecture Firms

	Important (Percent)	Satisfied (Percent)
Locational Features		
Proximity to business services	91	95
Proximity to where employees live	86	97
Proximity to restaurants/retail/personal services	85	94
Proximity to clients	79	96
Proximity to public transportation	55	92
General Building Features		
Rental rates (including pass-throughs/escalations)	92	89
Operating expenses	99	89
Image and prestige of the building	97	89
On-site parking	88	78
Tenant improvement allowance	91	77
Cost of parking	85	77
Environmentally friendly building systems and materials	91	82
Disabled access	76	79
Covered parking	59	73
Tenant mix	76	85
Features of Building Exterior		
Appearance of building	93	89
Appearance of grounds/landscaping	95	79
Outside signage for your organization	62	76
Outside loading docks	22	82
Operable windows	47	75
Roof-loading capacity	9	89
Features of Interior Common Areas		
Appearance of entry lobby (style/finishes)	99	74
Buildingwide security systems after hours	93	80
Appearance of common areas other than lobby	97	66
Elevator service speed	78	65
Buildingwide security systems during work day	76	82
Features of Tenants' Office Suites		
Comfortable temperature	99	73
Indoor air quality	99	81
Acoustics/noise control	99	77
Power capacity	95	90
Tenant control of temperature	99	72
Security/controlled access	86	82
Proximity to restrooms	90	94
Flexible suite layout (e.g., easily reconfigured)	91	83
Cost of after-hours heating/cooling	88	83
Proximity to elevators	73	90
Building Amenities		
Food service	50	73
Banking/ATM	52	76
Convenience retail stores	51	79
Fitness center	32	60
Child-care facility	33	69
Concierge	17	80
Shared videoconference facility	37	61
Shared teleconference facility	33	66
Shared business services (e.g., data and word processing)	24	73
Building Management		
Quality of building maintenance work	97	77
Building management's ability to meet your needs	96	82
Building management's responsiveness	95	80
Effectiveness of communications with building management	94	75
On-site building management staff	80	81
On-site security guard	64	77

Note: The numbers in the first column represent the percentage of respondents to whom a particular feature is important, the numbers in the second column the percentage of respondents who are satisfied with the feature as currently available.

Figure B-5

Importance of and Satisfaction with Building Features, Amenities, and Services for High-Tech Firms

	Important (Percent)	Satisfied (Percent)
Locational Features		
Proximity to business services	81	97
Proximity to where employees live	86	95
Proximity to restaurants/retail/personal services	79	96
Proximity to clients	71	98
Proximity to public transportation	79	96
General Building Features		
Rental rates (including pass-throughs/escalations)	88	83
Operating expenses	99	82
Image and prestige of the building	88	90
On-site parking	97	79
Tenant improvement allowance	94	80
Cost of parking	94	76
Environmentally friendly building systems and materials	86	89
Disabled access	72	87
Covered parking	72	71
Tenant mix	69	88
Features of Building Exterior		
Appearance of building	97	93
Appearance of grounds/landscaping	97	95
Outside signage for your organization	74	80
Outside loading docks	55	77
Operable windows	48	68
Roof-loading capacity	31	87
Features of Interior Common Areas		
Appearance of entry lobby (style/finishes)	92	86
Buildingwide security systems after hours	99	84
Appearance of common areas other than lobby	95	81
Elevator service speed	87	66
Buildingwide security systems during work day	90	80
Features of Tenants' Office Suites		
Comfortable temperature	95	70
Indoor air quality	94	78
Acoustics/noise control	98	82
Power capacity	99	87
Tenant control of temperature	98	62
Security/controlled access	97	88
Proximity to restrooms	93	93
Flexible suite layout (e.g., easily reconfigured)	96	88
Cost of after-hours heating/cooling	94	68
Proximity to elevators	82	97
Building Amenities		
Food service	83	69
Banking/ATM	73	65
Convenience retail stores	69	70
Fitness center	63	64
Child-care facility	56	62
Concierge	37	71
Shared videoconference facility	46	67
Shared teleconference facility	45	67
Shared business services (e.g., data and word processing)	37	81
Building Management		
Quality of building maintenance work	99	90
Building management's ability to meet your needs	99	92
Building management's responsiveness	99	86
Effectiveness of communications with building management	100	88
On-site building management staff	94	91
On-site security guard	97	82

Note: The numbers in the first column represent the percentage of respondents to whom a particular feature is important, the numbers in the second column the percentage of respondents who are satisfied with the feature as currently available.

Figure B-6 Importance of and Satisfaction with Building Features, Amenities, and Services for Communications Firms

	Important (Percent)	Satisfied (Percent)
Locational Features		
Proximity to business services	95	98
Proximity to where employees live	86	88
Proximity to restaurants/retail/personal services	85	96
Proximity to clients	82	93
Proximity to public transportation	78	98
General Building Features		
Rental rates (including pass-throughs/escalations)	99	84
Operating expenses	90	82
Image and prestige of the building	99	90
On-site parking	96	79
Tenant improvement allowance	96	84
Cost of parking	96	70
Environmentally friendly building systems and materials	95	87
Disabled access	72	94
Covered parking	85	79
Tenant mix	78	90
Features of Building Exterior		
Appearance of building	99	92
Appearance of grounds/landscaping	98	91
Outside signage for your organization	77	74
Outside loading docks	69	81
Operable windows	41	62
Roof-loading capacity	33	82
Features of Interior Common Areas		
Appearance of entry lobby (style/finishes)	91	93
Buildingwide security systems after hours	99	84
Appearance of common areas other than lobby	88	86
Elevator service speed	95	70
Buildingwide security systems during work day	97	82
Features of Tenants' Office Suites		
Comfortable temperature	96	78
Indoor air quality	99	77
Acoustics/noise control	98	83
Power capacity	98	88
Tenant control of temperature	97	74
Security/controlled access	97	91
Proximity to restrooms	95	93
Flexible suite layout (e.g., easily reconfigured)	97	87
Cost of after-hours heating/cooling	90	76
Proximity to elevators	89	97
Building Amenities		
Food service	80	74
Banking/ATM	82	84
Convenience retail stores	74	83
Fitness center	67	63
Child-care facility	47	51
Concierge	54	77
Shared videoconference facility	38	66
Shared teleconference facility	35	65
Shared business services (e.g., data and word processing)	33	77
Building Management		
Quality of building maintenance work	99	90
Building management's ability to meet your needs	99	92
Building management's responsiveness	99	86
Effectiveness of communications with building management	96	88
On-site building management staff	94	91
On-site security guard	97	82

Note: The numbers in the first column represent the percentage of respondents to whom a particular feature is important, the numbers in the second column the percentage of respondents who are satisfied with the feature as currently available.

Figure B-7

Importance of and Satisfaction with Building Features, Amenities, and Services for Insurance Firms

	Important (Percent)	Satisfied (Percent)
Locational Features		
Proximity to business services	80	97
Proximity to where employees live	81	93
Proximity to restaurants/retail/personal services	81	94
Proximity to clients	71	100
Proximity to public transportation	65	90
General Building Features		
Rental rates (including pass-throughs/escalations)	100	85
Operating expenses	100	86
Image and prestige of the building	98	94
On-site parking	98	81
Tenant improvement allowance	95	82
Cost of parking	86	71
Environmentally friendly building systems and materials	96	93
Disabled access	80	96
Covered parking	80	75
Tenant mix	76	94
Features of Building Exterior		
Appearance of building	98	99
Appearance of grounds/landscaping	98	96
Outside signage for your organization	78	69
Outside loading docks	62	73
Operable windows	37	66
Roof-loading capacity	25	91
Features of Interior Common Areas		
Appearance of entry lobby (style/finishes)	100	91
Buildingwide security systems after hours	100	81
Appearance of common areas other than lobby	100	84
Elevator service speed	93	76
Buildingwide security systems during work day	92	80
Features of Tenants' Office Suites		
Comfortable temperature	100	80
Indoor air quality	99	87
Acoustics/noise control	99	89
Power capacity	99	94
Tenant control of temperature	91	65
Security/controlled access	95	88
Proximity to restrooms	93	99
Flexible suite layout (e.g., easily reconfigured)	92	95
Cost of after-hours heating/cooling	91	79
Proximity to elevators	82	97
Building Amenities		
Food service	79	71
Banking/ATM	78	84
Convenience retail stores	65	80
Fitness center	55	57
Child-care facility	56	51
Concierge	37	69
Shared videoconference facility	46	63
Shared teleconference facility	43	71
Shared business services (e.g., data and word processing)	25	72
Building Management		
Quality of building maintenance work	100	90
Building management's ability to meet your needs	100	92
Building management's responsiveness	93	93
Effectiveness of communications with building management	99	89
On-site building management staff	99	94
On-site security guard	93	81

Note: The numbers in the first column represent the percentage of respondents to whom a particular feature is important, the numbers in the second column the percentage of respondents who are satisfied with the feature as currently available.

Figure B-8

Importance of and Satisfaction with Building Features, Amenities, and Services for Medical Services

	Important (Percent)	Satisfied (Percent)
Locational Features		
Proximity to business services	71	93
Proximity to where employees live	70	86
Proximity to restaurants/retail/personal services	65	92
Proximity to clients	83	97
Proximity to public transportation	83	93
General Building Features		
Rental rates (including pass-throughs/escalations)	99	77
Operating expenses	96	85
Image and prestige of the building	77	90
On-site parking	98	76
Tenant improvement allowance	99	76
Cost of parking	96	79
Environmentally friendly building systems and materials	91	86
Disabled access	95	87
Covered parking	80	73
Tenant mix	76	89
Features of Building Exterior		
Appearance of building	92	93
Appearance of grounds/landscaping	92	93
Outside signage for your organization	84	70
Outside loading docks	49	81
Operable windows	50	72
Roof-loading capacity	25	75
Features of Interior Common Areas		
Appearance of entry lobby (style/finishes)	99	87
Buildingwide security systems after hours	92	78
Appearance of common areas other than lobby	99	84
Elevator service speed	87	67
Buildingwide security systems during work day	89	78
Features of Tenants' Office Suites		
Comfortable temperature	100	65
Indoor air quality	96	75
Acoustics/noise control	94	77
Power capacity	97	71
Tenant control of temperature	99	57
Security/controlled access	99	86
Proximity to restrooms	95	91
Flexible suite layout (e.g., easily reconfigured)	94	86
Cost of after-hours heating/cooling	94	75
Proximity to elevators	90	93
Building Amenities		
Food service	71	64
Banking/ATM	62	78
Convenience retail stores	56	84
Fitness center	43	61
Child-care facility	40	54
Concierge	36	74
Shared videoconference facility	33	67
Shared teleconference facility	32	70
Shared business services (e.g., data and word processing)	35	77
Building Management		
Quality of building maintenance work	93	86
Building management's ability to meet your needs	100	85
Building management's responsiveness	100	87
Effectiveness of communications with building management	90	84
On-site building management staff	97	82
On-site security guard	92	76

Note: The numbers in the first column represent the percentage of respondents to whom a particular feature is important, the numbers in the second column the percentage of respondents who are satisfied with the feature as currently available.

Figure B-9 Importance of and Satisfaction with Building Features, Amenities, and Services for Nonprofit Organizations

	Important (Percent)	Satisfied (Percent)
Locational Features		
Proximity to business services	87	98
Proximity to where employees live	77	88
Proximity to restaurants/retail/personal services	81	94
Proximity to clients	68	73
Proximity to public transportation	87	95
General Building Features		
Rental rates (including pass-throughs/escalations)	99	82
Operating expenses	97	87
Image and prestige of the building	93	94
On-site parking	87	79
Tenant improvement allowance	92	83
Cost of parking	85	65
Environmentally friendly building systems and materials	92	88
Disabled access	82	98
Covered parking	75	84
Tenant mix	71	96
Features of Building Exterior		
Appearance of building	99	96
Appearance of grounds/landscaping	97	99
Outside signage for your organization	68	81
Outside loading docks	64	81
Operable windows	52	65
Roof-loading capacity	20	88
Features of Interior Common Areas		
Appearance of entry lobby (style/finishes)	99	97
Buildingwide security systems after hours	91	85
Appearance of common areas other than lobby	99	86
Elevator service speed	90	76
Buildingwide security systems during work day	95	82
Features of Tenants' Office Suites		
Comfortable temperature	100	74
Indoor air quality	96	83
Acoustics/noise control	95	80
Power capacity	97	93
Tenant control of temperature	93	54
Security/controlled access	97	92
Proximity to restrooms	97	97
Flexible suite layout (e.g., easily reconfigured)	89	81
Cost of after-hours heating/cooling	86	73
Proximity to elevators	86	86
Building Amenities		
Food service	67	71
Banking/ATM	69	81
Convenience retail stores	53	84
Fitness center	44	61
Child-care facility	41	51
Concierge	42	85
Shared videoconference facility	35	55
Shared teleconference facility	35	57
Shared business services (e.g., data and word processing)	23	73
Building Management		
Quality of building maintenance work	92	89
Building management's ability to meet your needs	93	96
Building management's responsiveness	92	92
Effectiveness of communications with building management	99	92
On-site building management staff	93	96
On-site security guard	93	88

Note: The numbers in the first column represent the percentage of respondents to whom a particular feature is important, the numbers in the second column the percentage of respondents who are satisfied with the feature as currently available.

Figure B-10

Importance of and Satisfaction with Building Features, Amenities, and Services for Retail Tenants

	Important (Percent)	Satisfied (Percent)
Locational Features		
Proximity to business services	82	95
Proximity to where employees live	67	67
Proximity to restaurants/retail/personal services	75	97
Proximity to clients	83	90
Proximity to public transportation	64	86
General Building Features		
Rental rates (including pass-throughs/escalations)	98	84
Operating expenses	87	87
Image and prestige of the building	95	94
On-site parking	94	71
Tenant improvement allowance	95	76
Cost of parking	87	65
Environmentally friendly building systems and materials	91	90
Disabled access	81	89
Covered parking	73	67
Tenant mix	78	91
Features of Building Exterior		
Appearance of building	95	94
Appearance of grounds/landscaping	98	94
Outside signage for your organization	85	77
Outside loading docks	66	74
Operable windows	37	76
Roof-loading capacity	24	84
Features of Interior Common Areas		
Appearance of entry lobby (style/finishes)	84	90
Buildingwide security systems after hours	95	85
Appearance of common areas other than lobby	87	90
Elevator service speed	75	82
Buildingwide security systems during work day	90	86
Features of Tenants' Office Suites		
Comfortable temperature	98	75
Indoor air quality	98	87
Acoustics/noise control	95	88
Power capacity	96	94
Tenant control of temperature	93	65
Security/controlled access	84	85
Proximity to restrooms	79	81
Flexible suite layout (e.g., easily reconfigured)	88	86
Cost of after-hours heating/cooling	83	73
Proximity to elevators	69	94
Building Amenities		
Food service	70	83
Banking/ATM	82	84
Convenience retail stores	70	86
Fitness center	47	70
Child-care facility	36	68
Concierge	49	80
Shared videoconference facility	25	79
Shared teleconference facility	26	79
Shared business services (e.g., data and word processing)	38	83
Building Management		
Quality of building maintenance work	94	89
Building management's ability to meet your needs	98	86
Building management's responsiveness	97	85
Effectiveness of communications with building management	91	89
On-site building management staff	89	88
On-site security guard	87	83

Note: The numbers in the first column represent the percentage of respondents to whom a particular feature is important, the numbers in the second column the percentage of respondents who are satisfied with the feature as currently available.

Figure B-11

Importance of and Satisfaction with Building Features, Amenities, and Services for Consulting Firms

	Important (Percent)	Satisfied (Percent)
Locational Features		
Proximity to business services	97	97
Proximity to where employees live	88	97
Proximity to restaurants/retail/personal services	85	90
Proximity to clients	81	100
Proximity to public transportation	78	89
General Building Features		
Rental rates (including pass-throughs/escalations)	100	97
Operating expenses	97	93
Image and prestige of the building	97	88
On-site parking	100	91
Tenant improvement allowance	93	85
Cost of parking	97	71
Environmentally friendly building systems and materials	97	87
Disabled access	80	81
Covered parking	100	79
Tenant mix	72	96
Features of Building Exterior		
Appearance of building	100	97
Appearance of grounds/landscaping	97	100
Outside signage for your organization	91	68
Outside loading docks	81	41
Operable windows	29	69
Roof-loading capacity	41	81
Features of Interior Common Areas		
Appearance of entry lobby (style/finishes)	100	97
Buildingwide security systems after hours	100	88
Appearance of common areas other than lobby	91	84
Elevator service speed	97	82
Buildingwide security systems during work day	97	82
Features of Tenants' Office Suites		
Comfortable temperature	100	67
Indoor air quality	100	79
Acoustics/noise control	100	76
Power capacity	100	84
Tenant control of temperature	97	81
Security/controlled access	97	97
Proximity to restrooms	94	97
Flexible suite layout (e.g., easily reconfigured)	100	81
Cost of after-hours heating/cooling	93	77
Proximity to elevators	94	97
Building Amenities		
Food service	97	77
Banking/ATM	84	82
Convenience retail stores	65	91
Fitness center	63	58
Child-care facility	50	40
Concierge	39	56
Shared videoconference facility	48	57
Shared teleconference facility	48	64
Shared business services (e.g., data and word processing)	43	71
Building Management		
Quality of building maintenance work	100	87
Building management's ability to meet your needs	100	91
Building management's responsiveness	100	91
Effectiveness of communications with building management	100	82
On-site building management staff	100	91
On-site security guard	100	87

Note: The numbers in the first column represent the percentage of respondents to whom a particular feature is important, the numbers in the second column the percentage of respondents who are satisfied with the feature as currently available.

Figure B-12

Importance of and Satisfaction with Building Features, Amenities, and Services for Government Agencies

	Important (Percent)	Satisfied (Percent)
Locational Features		
Proximity to business services	90	100
Proximity to where employees live	80	91
Proximity to restaurants/retail/personal services	83	91
Proximity to clients	77	96
Proximity to public transportation	90	98
General Building Features		
Rental rates (including pass-throughs/escalations)	94	95
Operating expenses	90	94
Image and prestige of the building	91	96
On-site parking	95	87
Tenant improvement allowance	92	85
Cost of parking	92	95
Environmentally friendly building systems and materials	97	91
Disabled access	98	95
Covered parking	77	92
Tenant mix	61	96
Features of Building Exterior		
Appearance of building	98	95
Appearance of grounds/landscaping	98	95
Outside signage for your organization	74	88
Outside loading docks	71	83
Operable windows	41	83
Roof-loading capacity	36	87
Features of Interior Common Areas		
Appearance of entry lobby (style/finishes)	97	92
Buildingwide security systems after hours	98	93
Appearance of common areas other than lobby	98	88
Elevator service speed	93	76
Buildingwide security systems during work day	93	97
Features of Tenants' Office Suites		
Comfortable temperature	98	80
Indoor air quality	100	88
Acoustics/noise control	98	93
Power capacity	100	95
Tenant control of temperature	93	66
Security/controlled access	98	91
Proximity to restrooms	95	95
Flexible suite layout (e.g., easily reconfigured)	95	90
Cost of after-hours heating/cooling	84	86
Proximity to elevators	92	98
Building Amenities		
Food service	85	80
Banking/ATM	68	87
Convenience retail stores	65	81
Fitness center	61	65
Child-care facility	60	57
Concierge	48	91
Shared videoconference facility	43	81
Shared teleconference facility	43	83
Shared business services (e.g., data and word processing)	24	79
Building Management		
Quality of building maintenance work	97	93
Building management's ability to meet your needs	98	95
Building management's responsiveness	98	97
Effectiveness of communications with building management	93	95
On-site building management staff	93	97
On-site security guard	95	93

Note: The numbers in the first column represent the percentage of respondents to whom a particular feature is important, the numbers in the second column the percentage of respondents who are satisfied with the feature as currently available.

Figure B-13

Importance of and Satisfaction with Building Features, Amenities, and Services for Engineering Firms

	Important (Percent)	Satisfied (Percent)
Locational Features		
Proximity to business services	90	100
Proximity to where employees live	93	98
Proximity to restaurants/retail/personal services	83	95
Proximity to clients	81	96
Proximity to public transportation	66	93
General Building Features		
Rental rates (including pass-throughs/escalations)	97	79
Operating expenses	97	91
Image and prestige of the building	91	93
On-site parking	95	82
Tenant improvement allowance	89	84
Cost of parking	91	74
Environmentally friendly building systems and materials	84	94
Disabled access	78	93
Covered parking	68	82
Tenant mix	72	92
Features of Building Exterior		
Appearance of building	98	93
Appearance of grounds/landscaping	98	93
Outside signage for your organization	76	76
Outside loading docks	59	78
Operable windows	44	83
Roof-loading capacity	17	82
Features of Interior Common Areas		
Appearance of entry lobby (style/finishes)	95	93
Buildingwide security systems after hours	95	88
Appearance of common areas other than lobby	95	89
Elevator service speed	82	81
Buildingwide security systems during work day	81	89
Features of Tenants' Office Suites		
Comfortable temperature	97	84
Indoor air quality	98	81
Acoustics/noise control	98	89
Power capacity	98	100
Tenant control of temperature	94	64
Security/controlled access	95	94
Proximity to restrooms	96	93
Flexible suite layout (e.g., easily reconfigured)	91	89
Cost of after-hours heating/cooling	96	74
Proximity to elevators	85	100
Building Amenities		
Food service	80	73
Banking/ATM	67	72
Convenience retail stores	65	78
Fitness center	64	63
Child-care facility	43	57
Concierge	33	79
Shared videoconference facility	50	61
Shared teleconference facility	48	69
Shared business services (e.g., data and word processing)	33	78
Building Management		
Quality of building maintenance work	85	89
Building management's ability to meet your needs	82	95
Building management's responsiveness	84	93
Effectiveness of communications with building management	98	85
On-site building management staff	87	89
On-site security guard	87	75

Note: The numbers in the first column represent the percentage of respondents to whom a particular feature is important, the numbers in the second column the percentage of respondents who are satisfied with the feature as currently available.

Figure B-14 Importance of and Satisfaction with Building Features, Amenities, and Services for Accounting Firms

	Important (Percent)	Satisfied (Percent)
Locational Features		
Proximity to business services	96	100
Proximity to where employees live	85	98
Proximity to restaurants/retail/personal services	83	93
Proximity to clients	85	98
Proximity to public transportation	73	98
General Building Features		
Rental rates (including pass-throughs/escalations)	100	93
Operating expenses	98	93
Image and prestige of the building	96	86
On-site parking	89	68
Tenant improvement allowance	92	88
Cost of parking	91	80
Environmentally friendly building systems and materials	91	91
Disabled access	66	92
Covered parking	81	65
Tenant mix	77	95
Features of Building Exterior		
Appearance of building	98	91
Appearance of grounds/landscaping	96	89
Outside signage for your organization	63	83
Outside loading docks	41	85
Operable windows	32	72
Roof-loading capacity	10	89
Features of Interior Common Areas		
Appearance of entry lobby (style/finishes)	96	83
Buildingwide security systems after hours	96	89
Appearance of common areas other than lobby	98	87
Elevator service speed	91	77
Buildingwide security systems during work day	89	91
Features of Tenants' Office Suites		
Comfortable temperature	98	77
Indoor air quality	98	81
Acoustics/noise control	96	79
Power capacity	98	92
Tenant control of temperature	98	67
Security/controlled access	94	91
Proximity to restrooms	91	98
Flexible suite layout (e.g., easily reconfigured)	83	92
Cost of after-hours heating/cooling	90	82
Proximity to elevators	84	83
Building Amenities		
Food service	74	69
Banking/ATM	65	66
Convenience retail stores	58	82
Fitness center	47	67
Child-care facility	32	58
Concierge	49	82
Shared videoconference facility	32	79
Shared teleconference facility	23	74
Shared business services (e.g., data and word processing)	19	81
Building Management		
Quality of building maintenance work	98	91
Building management's ability to meet your needs	94	89
Building management's responsiveness	94	89
Effectiveness of communications with building management	91	85
On-site building management staff	96	89
On-site security guard	96	84

Note: The numbers in the first column represent the percentage of respondents to whom a particular feature is important, the numbers in the second column the percentage of respondents who are satisfied with the feature as currently available.

Figure B-15

Importance of and Satisfaction with Building Features, Amenities, and Services for Construction Firms

	Important (Percent)	Satisfied (Percent)
Locational Features		
Proximity to business services	78	91
Proximity to where employees live	78	96
Proximity to restaurants/retail/personal services	48	95
Proximity to clients	65	68
Proximity to public transportation	26	86
General Building Features		
Rental rates (including pass-throughs/escalations)	95	90
Operating expenses	91	91
Image and prestige of the building	95	95
On-site parking	95	91
Tenant improvement allowance	82	83
Cost of parking	85	95
Environmentally friendly building systems and materials	57	90
Disabled access	67	95
Covered parking	45	83
Tenant mix	30	90
Features of Building Exterior		
Appearance of building	71	90
Appearance of grounds/landscaping	95	86
Outside signage for your organization	64	71
Outside loading docks	45	94
Operable windows	33	84
Roof-loading capacity	24	94
Features of Interior Common Areas		
Appearance of entry lobby (style/finishes)	95	82
Buildingwide security systems after hours	91	95
Appearance of common areas other than lobby	95	91
Elevator service speed	72	75
Buildingwide security systems during work day	84	77
Features of Tenants' Office Suites		
Comfortable temperature	100	52
Indoor air quality	82	67
Acoustics/noise control	91	67
Power capacity	95	95
Tenant control of temperature	100	55
Security/controlled access	75	74
Proximity to restrooms	91	95
Flexible suite layout (e.g., easily reconfigured)	81	79
Cost of after-hours heating/cooling	90	88
Proximity to elevators	71	93
Building Amenities		
Food service	55	69
Banking/ATM	30	87
Convenience retail stores	38	100
Fitness center	50	80
Child-care facility	25	79
Concierge	16	86
Shared videoconference facility	25	85
Shared teleconference facility	25	85
Shared business services (e.g., data and word processing)	20	85
Building Management		
Quality of building maintenance work	95	90
Building management's ability to meet your needs	90	75
Building management's responsiveness	85	75
Effectiveness of communications with building management	86	67
On-site building management staff	90	76
On-site security guard	48	88

Note: The numbers in the first column represent the percentage of respondents to whom a particular feature is important, the numbers in the second column the percentage of respondents who are satisfied with the feature as currently available.

Figure B-16

Importance of and Satisfaction with Building Features, Amenities, and Services for Utilities

	Important (Percent)	Satisfied (Percent)
Locational Features		
Proximity to business services	92	91
Proximity to where employees live	85	83
Proximity to restaurants/retail/personal services	77	83
Proximity to clients	85	100
Proximity to public transportation	77	92
General Building Features		
Rental rates (including pass-throughs/escalations)	100	92
Operating expenses	100	92
Image and prestige of the building	83	92
On-site parking	100	58
Tenant improvement allowance	80	75
Cost of parking	92	75
Environmentally friendly building systems and materials	100	83
Disabled access	83	91
Covered parking	92	64
Tenant mix	91	100
Features of Building Exterior		
Appearance of building	100	92
Appearance of grounds/landscaping	100	67
Outside signage for your organization	83	70
Outside loading docks	75	60
Operable windows	45	67
Roof-loading capacity	45	86
Features of Interior Common Areas		
Appearance of entry lobby (style/finishes)	100	83
Buildingwide security systems after hours	92	67
Appearance of common areas other than lobby	100	83
Elevator service speed	92	75
Buildingwide security systems during work day	92	58
Features of Tenants' Office Suites		
Comfortable temperature	100	83
Indoor air quality	100	92
Acoustics/noise control	100	92
Power capacity	100	100
Tenant control of temperature	83	73
Security/controlled access	92	75
Proximity to restrooms	83	92
Flexible suite layout (e.g., easily reconfigured)	92	92
Cost of after-hours heating/cooling	83	82
Proximity to elevators	75	92
Building Amenities		
Food service	83	92
Banking/ATM	92	92
Convenience retail stores	67	73
Fitness center	64	67
Child-care facility	54	71
Concierge	45	75
Shared videoconference facility	33	87
Shared teleconference facility	50	100
Shared business services (e.g., data and word processing)	27	88
Building Management		
Quality of building maintenance work	100	100
Building management's ability to meet your needs	100	92
Building management's responsiveness	100	92
Effectiveness of communications with building management	100	82
On-site building management staff	92	100
On-site security guard	100	64

Note: The numbers in the first column represent the percentage of respondents to whom a particular feature is important, the numbers in the second column the percentage of respondents who are satisfied with the feature as currently available.

Figure B-17

Importance of and Satisfaction with Building Features, Amenities, and Services for Transportation Companies

	Important (Percent)	Satisfied (Percent)
Locational Features		
Proximity to business services	84	100
Proximity to where employees live	76	83
Proximity to restaurants/retail/personal services	80	100
Proximity to clients	58	100
Proximity to public transportation	69	100
General Building Features		
Rental rates (including pass-throughs/escalations)	100	92
Operating expenses	96	80
Image and prestige of the building	92	100
On-site parking	92	79
Tenant improvement allowance	96	83
Cost of parking	85	64
Environmentally friendly building systems and materials	88	96
Disabled access	73	96
Covered parking	73	64
Tenant mix	88	92
Features of Building Exterior		
Appearance of building	96	100
Appearance of grounds/landscaping	96	96
Outside signage for your organization	54	78
Outside loading docks	52	83
Operable windows	22	82
Roof-loading capacity	8	96
Features of Interior Common Areas		
Appearance of entry lobby (style/finishes)	100	92
Buildingwide security systems after hours	100	88
Appearance of common areas other than lobby	96	92
Elevator service speed	85	77
Buildingwide security systems during work day	88	81
Features of Tenants' Office Suites		
Comfortable temperature	96	58
Indoor air quality	96	65
Acoustics/noise control	100	88
Power capacity	96	92
Tenant control of temperature	96	58
Security/controlled access	96	92
Proximity to restrooms	92	100
Flexible suite layout (e.g., easily reconfigured)	92	87
Cost of after-hours heating/cooling	87	83
Proximity to elevators	77	96
Building Amenities		
Food service	79	82
Banking/ATM	54	91
Convenience retail stores	62	77
Fitness center	46	83
Child-care facility	25	73
Concierge	39	86
Shared videoconference facility	39	79
Shared teleconference facility	33	85
Shared business services (e.g., data and word processing)	28	60
Building Management		
Quality of building maintenance work	100	81
Building management's ability to meet your needs	100	81
Building management's responsiveness	100	81
Effectiveness of communications with building management	100	81
On-site building management staff	88	85
On-site security guard	88	69

Note: The numbers in the first column represent the percentage of respondents to whom a particular feature is important, the numbers in the second column the percentage of respondents who are satisfied with the feature as currently available.

Figure B-18

Importance of and Satisfaction with Building Features, Amenities, and Services for Manufacturing Companies

	Important (Percent)	Satisfied (Percent)
Locational Features		
Proximity to business services	77	97
Proximity to where employees live	71	86
Proximity to restaurants/retail/personal services	69	93
Proximity to clients	50	89
Proximity to public transportation	50	91
General Building Features		
Rental rates (including pass-throughs/escalations)	91	92
Operating expenses	94	87
Image and prestige of the building	93	93
On-site parking	97	84
Tenant improvement allowance	76	85
Cost of parking	88	85
Environmentally friendly building systems and materials	97	90
Disabled access	83	90
Covered parking	67	69
Tenant mix	73	96
Features of Building Exterior		
Appearance of building	97	97
Appearance of grounds/landscaping	97	94
Outside signage for your organization	82	83
Outside loading docks	73	82
Operable windows	23	54
Roof-loading capacity	24	87
Features of Interior Common Areas		
Appearance of entry lobby (style/finishes)	94	100
Buildingwide security systems after hours	94	87
Appearance of common areas other than lobby	95	91
Elevator service speed	78	65
Buildingwide security systems during work day	83	86
Features of Tenants' Office Suites		
Comfortable temperature	97	73
Indoor air quality	97	88
Acoustics/noise control	94	91
Power capacity	86	87
Tenant control of temperature	97	73
Security/controlled access	80	84
Proximity to restrooms	86	93
Flexible suite layout (e.g., easily reconfigured)	89	91
Cost of after-hours heating/cooling	91	80
Proximity to elevators	64	93
Building Amenities		
Food service	67	82
Banking/ATM	60	85
Convenience retail stores	50	88
Fitness center	31	65
Child-care facility	23	68
Concierge	26	81
Shared videoconference facility	30	65
Shared teleconference facility	30	75
Shared business services (e.g., data and word processing)	15	75
Building Management		
Quality of building maintenance work	94	85
Building management's ability to meet your needs	93	91
Building management's responsiveness	94	91
Effectiveness of communications with building management	92	89
On-site building management staff	78	93
On-site security guard	71	89

Note: The numbers in the first column represent the percentage of respondents to whom a particular feature is important, the numbers in the second column the percentage of respondents who are satisfied with the feature as currently available.

Figure B-19

Importance of and Satisfaction with Building Features, Amenities, and Services for Oil and Gas Companies

	Important (Percent)	Satisfied (Percent)
Locational Features		
Proximity to business services	98	86
Proximity to where employees live	86	92
Proximity to restaurants/retail/personal services	89	98
Proximity to clients	98	89
Proximity to public transportation	75	95
General Building Features		
Rental rates (including pass-throughs/escalations)	100	83
Operating expenses	98	87
Image and prestige of the building	97	94
On-site parking	95	80
Tenant improvement allowance	97	81
Cost of parking	93	76
Environmentally friendly building systems and materials	94	93
Disabled access	77	98
Covered parking	85	81
Tenant mix	79	95
Features of Building Exterior		
Appearance of building	100	95
Appearance of grounds/landscaping	98	95
Outside signage for your organization	63	81
Outside loading docks	48	86
Operable windows	44	75
Roof-loading capacity	19	86
Features of Interior Common Areas		
Appearance of entry lobby (style/finishes)	100	86
Buildingwide security systems after hours	88	98
Appearance of common areas other than lobby	87	77
Elevator service speed	90	69
Buildingwide security systems during work day	87	88
Features of Tenants' Office Suites		
Comfortable temperature	100	74
Indoor air quality	98	80
Acoustics/noise control	100	77
Power capacity	98	93
Tenant control of temperature	97	63
Security/controlled access	97	86
Proximity to restrooms	97	98
Flexible suite layout (e.g., easily reconfigured)	93	83
Cost of after-hours heating/cooling	89	79
Proximity to elevators	84	98
Building Amenities		
Food service	77	78
Banking/ATM	64	89
Convenience retail stores	64	80
Fitness center	64	68
Child-care fac ility	37	67
Concierge	43	77
Shared videoconference facility	45	72
Shared teleconference facility	43	71
Shared business services (e.g., data and word processing)	31	76
Building Management		
Quality of building maintenance work	100	94
Building management's ability to meet your needs	100	94
Building management's responsiveness	100	91
Effectiveness of communications with building management	98	95
On-site building management staff	98	92
On-site security guard	92	85

Note: The numbers in the first column represent the percentage of respondents to whom a particular feature is important, the numbers in the second column the percentage of respondents who are satisfied with the feature as currently available.

Figure B-20

Importance of and Satisfaction with Building Features, Amenities, and Services for Employment Agencies

	Important (Percent)	Satisfied (Percent)
Locational Features		
Proximity to business services	93	98
Proximity to where employees live	89	100
Proximity to restaurants/retail/personal services	87	85
Proximity to clients	84	100
Proximity to public transportation	78	85
General Building Features		
Rental rates (including pass-throughs/escalations)	100	88
Operating expenses	97	86
Image and prestige of the building	98	87
On-site parking	96	73
Tenant improvement allowance	97	83
Cost of parking	93	72
Environmentally friendly building systems and materials	86	86
Disabled access	88	88
Covered parking	80	74
Tenant mix	68	90
Features of Building Exterior		
Appearance of building	98	93
Appearance of grounds/landscaping	96	93
Outside signage for your organization	76	66
Outside loading docks	57	82
Operable windows	33	62
Roof-loading capacity	18	78
Features of Interior Common Areas		
Appearance of entry lobby (style/finishes)	98	87
Buildingwide security systems after hours	98	84
Appearance of common areas other than lobby	98	87
Elevator service speed	85	75
Buildingwide security systems during work day	91	77
Features of Tenants' Office Suites		
Comfortable temperature	98	69
Indoor air quality	100	80
Acoustics/noise control	100	81
Power capacity	95	91
Tenant control of temperature	93	50
Security/controlled access	84	81
Proximity to restrooms	89	100
Flexible suite layout (e.g., easily reconfigured)	89	87
Cost of after-hours heating/cooling	88	74
Proximity to elevators	80	96
Building Amenities		
Food service	82	70
Banking/ATM	71	67
Convenience retail stores	67	64
Fitness center	59	41
Child-care facility	41	64
Concierge	50	65
Shared videoconference facility	36	56
Shared teleconference facility	20	50
Shared business services (e.g., data and word processing)	21	62
Building Management		
Quality of building maintenance work	98	91
Building management's ability to meet your needs	98	87
Building management's responsiveness	98	89
Effectiveness of communications with building management	98	87
On-site building management staff	98	89
On-site security guard	93	83

Note: The numbers in the first column represent the percentage of respondents to whom a particular feature is important, the numbers in the second column the percentage of respondents who are satisfied with the feature as currently available.

Figure B-21

Importance of and Satisfaction with Building Features, Amenities, and Services for Other Firms

	Important (Percent)	Satisfied (Percent)
Locational Features		
Proximity to business services	80	98
Proximity to where employees live	76	92
Proximity to restaurants/retail/personal services	71	94
Proximity to clients	73	97
Proximity to public transportation	64	91
General Building Features		
Rental rates (including pass-throughs/escalations)	95	90
Operating expenses	93	83
Image and prestige of the building	98	92
On-site parking	95	83
Tenant improvement allowance	94	80
Cost of parking	91	76
Environmentally friendly building systems and materials	91	92
Disabled access	78	94
Covered parking	75	83
Tenant mix	69	90
Features of Building Exterior		
Appearance of building	96	91
Appearance of grounds/landscaping	95	88
Outside signage for your organization	67	83
Outside loading docks	59	76
Operable windows	40	66
Roof-loading capacity	19	84
Features of Interior Common Areas		
Appearance of entry lobby (style/finishes)	97	89
Buildingwide security systems after hours	97	86
Appearance of common areas other than lobby	98	82
Elevator service speed	86	54
Buildingwide security systems during work day	91	85
Features of Tenants' Office Suites		
Comfortable temperature	96	71
Indoor air quality	93	80
Acoustics/noise control	100	80
Power capacity	96	96
Tenant control of temperature	99	65
Security/controlled access	93	89
Proximity to restrooms	97	93
Flexible suite layout (e.g., easily reconfigured)	94	81
Cost of after-hours heating/cooling	88	76
Proximity to elevators	91	98
Building Amenities		
Food service	75	70
Banking/ATM	66	73
Convenience retail stores	60	79
Fitness center	49	53
Child-care facility	42	47
Concierge	43	75
Shared videoconference facility	34	65
Shared teleconference facility	23	64
Shared business services (e.g., data and word processing)	22	69
Building Management		
Quality of building maintenance work	92	85
Building management's ability to meet your needs	94	86
Building management's responsiveness	99	89
Effectiveness of communications with building management	88	84
On-site building management staff	94	87
On-site security guard	90	80

Note: The numbers in the first column represent the percentage of respondents to whom a particular feature is important, the numbers in the second column the percentage of respondents who are satisfied with the feature as currently available.